AN INTRODUCTION TO

POTTERY

A STEP-BY-STEP PROJECT BOOK

AN INTRODUCTION TO
POTTERY
A STEP-BY-STEP PROJECT BOOK

LINDE WALLNER

TRANSLATED BY C. J. McLEOD

CHARTWELL
BOOKS, INC.

A QUINTET BOOK

Published by Chartwell Books
A Division of Book Sales, Inc.
110 Enterprise Avenue
Secaucus, New Jersey 07094

ISBN 1-55521-453-3

This book was designed and produced by
Quintet Publishing Limited
6 Blundell Street
London N7 9BH

Creative Director: Peter Bridgewater
Art Director: Ian Hunt
Designer: Sally McKay
Project Editor: Sally Harper
Editor: Richard Rosenfeld

Typeset in Great Britain by
Central Southern Typesetters, Eastbourne
Manufactured in Hong Kong by
Regent Publishing Services Limited
Printed in Hong Kong by
Kwong Fat Offset Printing Company Limited

CONTENTS

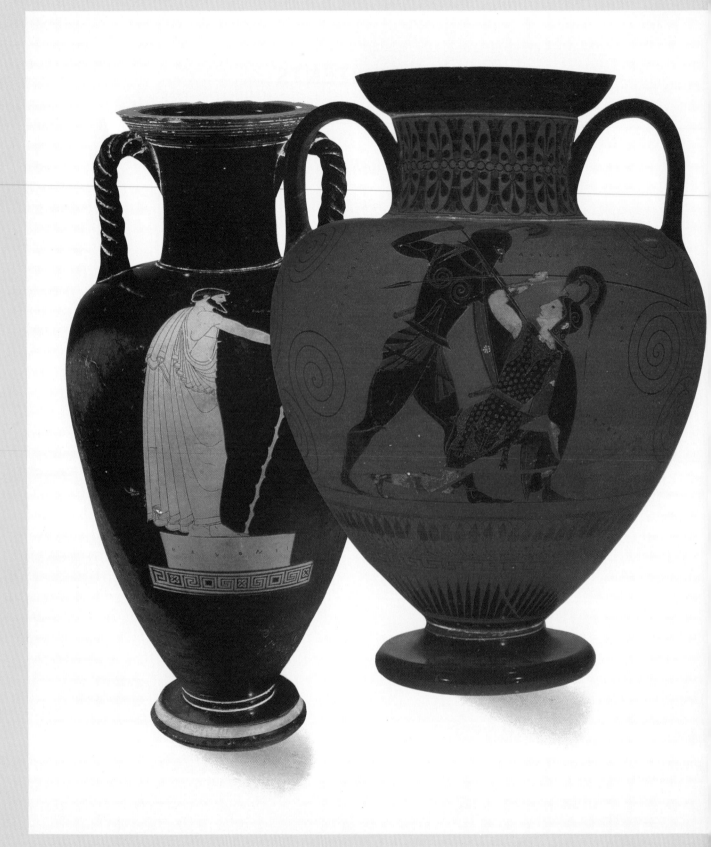

Introduction

Clay – an ancient material

◆ · · · ◆ · · · ◆ · · · ◆ · · · ◆ · · · ◆ · · · ◆

Pottery can be traced back as far as the 7th century BC, with potters probably being the first of all craftsmen. Amongst the earliest finds are artistic figures, images of people and animals, and household implements including beakers and dishes. In 3,600 BC the first potter's wheels were used in Mesopotamia. These wheels do not bear comparison with those of today, and were aids to highly symmetrical works. Egyptian potters used the first foot wheels, and developed the first glazes. Interestingly, the first foot wheels were spindle wheels constructed according to the same principle as those used for the modern version.

RIGHT: **A pot from Niger, decorated with slips and pigments. It is a contemporary pot, but traditional in style and symbolic decoration.**

The wide trade in pieces of pottery, for instance along the Silk Road from the Far East to China, meant similar techniques and patterns occurred in many places, periods and cultures. In fact entire ages can be divided and named after ceramic patterns and shapes – ribbon ware, the geometric age, and so on. The best-preserved ceramics are burial objects found in graves. They provide us with an accurate picture of society through the ages.

A brief history

◆ · · · ◆ · · · ◆ · · · ◆ · · · ◆ · · · ◆ · · · ◆

THE NEAR EAST

The natural oases of the near East had been settled since 7 BC by New Stone Age rural groups. Near Jericho, in Palestine, the oldest known ceramic objects were found. The finds of Hacilar, in Anatolia, are slightly more recent, dating from the 6th century BC. These early finds were shaped by hand, and constructed from a basic round form. The first vessels are decorated, and include simple etched patterns, stripes, zigzags, and diamonds. Clay slip of a contrasting colour was used for painting or colouring – red, yellow-white, grey or black-brown, according to the type of clay.

The early potters polished the surface of ceramics with pebbles. This technique not only produced a smooth surface, but made the exterior thicker, enabling it to hold water. The third effect of this process was a shiny matt surface. The centre of this early period was in the country that we know today as Iran.

Up to the middle of the 5th century BC, Samara ware was emerging in northern Mesopotamia (the product is named after its place of origin). Equally fascinating pieces can be found in other parts of Mesopotamia. Looking more closely at them, it is clear that these are no ordinary pieces, but have a cult status. Among the most beautiful works in this area are the ceramics from Susa, in the eastern border area of Mesopotamia. Susa was probably not only the centre of the ceramic industry, but also a trade centre for distribution of religious and secular vessels.

In the 4th century BC thin-walled, elegantly shaped dishes, beakers, vases and goblets of varying size began to appear. Susa was also where the first classical style developed, producing exquisite pieces of ceramic. Geometrical patterns appear side by side with stylized human figures and animals, and floral decorations were widely used. The colours of the decorations are red or black. By using the potter's wheel, many years later, potters again attained similar skills to those of the Samara period. Incidentally, the ceramics were made watertight by using a high firing temperature. Ceramics from Susa are collected in the Louvre.

More evidence of a highly developed culture exists in small clay tablets found in Uruk, south Mesopotamia, which date from the 3rd century BC. These tablets bear the oldest, if not always legible signs of writing. However, after a 'golden age' of ceramics followed a much quieter period. In turn, this was followed by another creative period.

CHINA

Before turning to the development of ceramic objects found in Europe, let us look at eastern Asia where the potter's craft developed more rapidly than in any other area.

RIGHT: **Earthenware figure placed in a tomb as a guardian, Tang dynasty.**

The earliest traces of the Chinese people date back to the New Stone Age. Chinese ceramics can be dated to this period too. Evidence of these neolithic cultures is provided by ceramics from significant production centres of the 5th century BC, which were found as burial objects. The centres of these neolithic cultures are divided, according to ceramics, into three main groups: west China, east coast China, and south China.

On the east coast, as early as the 3rd century BC, there were unpainted grey-black ceramics turned on a potter's wheel. The wheel was also known in south China. The products were decorated either by scratching or string.

The cultures in west China produced thin pieces of ceramics, mostly urns or burial objects, produced for the cult of the dead. As early as the 1st century BC these master potters used a simple feldspar glaze. This was the first step on the long road to the manufacture of porcelain, with which the Chinese potters achieved their real glory. It is estimated that porcelain was already being manufactured in the 7th century AD. The first porcelain was probably fired in the same kiln as the ceramics of the Sung period (960–1279). This ware was called Ding-Yao, and it was very delicately shaped, coated with cream-coloured glaze, and given an incised or imprinted decoration.

State sponsorship enabled more ambitious and more varied works to be produced. The potters fired the thin-walled plates and dishes upside-down, the unglazed edge was covered with silver leaf, copper leaf or gold leaf, and it was protected against knocks. Our gold-rimmed crockery may well stem from this tradition.

Real porcelain production began during the Ming dynasty (1368–1644).

LEFT: **Qing dynasty porcelain vase decorated in famille rose enamels.**

The typical blue decoration of Chinese porcelain goes back to Islamic influences. In the mid-14th century huge caravans moved along the Silk Road from the near East to China. The emperor's court sponsored brilliant products, and trade flourished. New developments in glaze led to new decorations: red, green, and yellow were used as well as cobalt blue. Small bridges, similar to enamel, prevented the colours from running. Chinese porcelain production peaked under Emperor Kang-Hi (1672–1722). In Europe, the markets demanded 'white gold', and therefore entire shiploads of porcelain made their way around the Cape of Good Hope to Europe. The porcelain was carefully manufactured and was of the highest quality. Until the 18th century production increased sharply, resulting in some loss of quality, eventually leading to today's mass-produced products.

JAPAN

Human and ceramic development followed a very similar path in Japan. Ceramic finds from the neolithic period have string decorations, etched patterns, and simple paintings applied with earth-coloured material. From the 4th to the 6th century Haniwa figures appeared. They are typically Japanese, and do not occur in other early cultures. At the beginning of the 5th century the Chinese influence became very clear. The real significance of Japanese ceramics appeared only with the che-no-yu tea ceremony from the end of the 16th century onwards. The plain simplicity of the ware was ideally suited to the tea masters (interestingly, if a ceramic piece which was considered beautiful and venerable was broken, it was repaired carefully with gold lacquer). The Japanese too turned their attentions towards Europe and exported huge amounts of mass-produced pottery and imitations of classic pieces.

There existed only a few small factories which maintained the tradition. In 1930, however, a new development took place and modern, typically Japanese ceramics were produced. They avoided plain simplicity and unnecessary decoration. Contemporary European ceramics follow this tradition.

GREECE

Heat, water, and fertile, arable land around Thessalonika meant the region was settled from a very early period, as was the island of Crete, which was probably also a stopping-off point for Egyptians on the way to Europe. Greece produced the oldest culture on European soil. From as early as the 4th century BC we know of grey-black vessels, which were coated with a ceramic varnish made from vegetable juice. The first figures were corpulent clay idols, part of a matriarchal divinity. They stem from Crete and are the beginning of Minoan culture. The sub-neolithic period at the turn of the 4th and 3rd century BC is characterized by grey-red-black ceramics, which are incized and incorporate a polished pattern. Painted vessels occur around the end of the 3rd century BC.

The Ancient Greeks, or Minoans, knew the secret of reduction firing. Metal oxide fired in a deoxygenated atmosphere produces a change of colour. The Anatolian and Egyptian influences indicate a flourishing trade. The destruction of Crete, which was probably caused by the eruption of a volcano on Thera (Santorini), brought these early Minoan cultures to an end. The few relics of this period include lipped pots, teapots, huge storage jars, vases and dishes, some of which have been found under thick layers of ash. These finds enable us to paint an accurate picture of Minoan culture. Consequently we know, for example, what was eaten and drunk, because the porous shards of the storage vessels absorbed liquids. Also surviving from this period are clay tablets with writing, and entire inventories. Inscriptions are also to be found on pots from the palace of Kadmos, in Thebes. These are the oldest known texts of the mainland.

At an early stage the Greeks began to decorate their containers. Their patterns crop up everywhere in Greece, with

ABOVE: **Athenian white-ground lekythos (funerary oil container), late 5th century BC.**

small time lapses, from the islands to the mainland. Mainland pottery was superior to that of the islands, being more durable, thinner, and shiny. The shape was, however, identical to that of the island pottery. In the ancient city of Tanagra are small painted female Tanagra figures. From the late Minoan age date wavy lines, spirals, dotted rosettes, double-headed axes (some of which appear alongside natural decorations), olive branches, leaves, lilies, reeds, and other types of Cretan flora appearing on vases, dishes, and beakers.

At a later date this style changed into the marine, which features starfish, octopi, dolphins, and marine fauna. This marine style was superseded by a return to simple, often abstract decoration, whose naturalistic origin was hardly recognizable. Meanwhile, on the mainland entire stories were depicted on containers. Yet with the decline of the Mycenean rule came a parallel decline in ceramics. Later in Athens, in the geometric age, we again find meandering patterns, zigzags, angles, rhombi, and spirals on dishes and vases.

Corinthian and Attic potters competed with each other. The Corinthians followed the geometric style with depictions of animals and plant decorations. In Attica figurative representations were also used in geometric decoration. The Periclean age resulted in a flood of ceramics. Vase decorations included fawns, young women, athletes, animals, and entire hunting scenes. Pots from present day Greece reveal few new influences.

ETRURIA

Little is known of the Etruscans, although we believe they are an offshoot of the Greeks. Perhaps Aeneas, fleeing from Agamemnon, was one of the forefathers. This would also explain the strong Greek influence on Etruscan ceramics. Greek works of art and ceramics were traded in the 7th century BC across the Mediterranean. Since no marble was available in Etruria, a relatively large amount of terracotta has been found there. Later, in the 3rd century BC, Rome came to power and the importance of Etruria declined.

ROME

The Romans took from the Greeks not only their gods (which they renamed), architectural styles and sculpture, but

BELOW: **The Creation of Pandora, an Athenian red-figure vase painting from the early 5th century BC.**

techniques of ceramic manufacture. Because the Roman Empire was very large, incorporating many varied tribes, there were many varied types of ceramics. One of the commonest was *terra sigillata,* a sealed type of earth pot also made in the east Mediterranean. The technique involved delicately washed red aluminium oxide being fired at a great heat and coated with a wafer-thin glaze. These ceramics were often decorated with a relief pattern, and the clay was pressed into shaping bowls with rollers or punches. Reliefs were cut into these shapes and the soft clay was produced. Through shrinkage, occurring during the drying stage, the potters were able to remove the shaping bowls with ease. In this way series production became possible.

There were large factories in southern France at Toulouse, in north Africa, and on the Rhine. The beautiful, fine pieces produced there were mainly used as tableware. In addition to such items, rough, coarse earthenware pieces were made, to be used as basic crockery and for storage. In the 1st century simple lead glazes first appeared.

Wherever we find Roman remains, there is not only crockery, but also a vast number of lamps left behind by Roman potters. These simple oil lamps found across the Roman Empire originally had heathen, then Christian motifs. Other frequent discoveries include elaborately decorated masks and terracotta pieces.

THE NEW WORLD

In the ancient civilizations of Latin America we again come across ceramic finds at a very early stage. The oldest products date from the 4th century BC and were manufactured in Ecuador.

The ceramic patterns and shapes give us an informative picture of this early Peruvian period. In the Chavin period, which coincides with the Roman Empire, sculptures and painted vessels were a ritual element, being used principally for religious purposes. Clay vessels, animal figures, and all kinds of musical instruments have survived as burial gifts. The vessels were often so-called stirrup vessels, or were given birds' beaks as spouts. Animals and people also appear in vessel form. The dishes and vessels were etched and painted cold. These decorations are symbols and signs similar to those found everywhere at the beginning of human civilization – lozenges, spirals, sun signs, crosses and zigzags. Despite the differences between North and South America, common characteristics can be seen, albeit over long periods of time.

The advanced civilizations of Mexico and Peru made ceramic masterpieces, using the most basic resources. Since the ancient people of Latin America did not have the potter's wheel, ceramics were built up and shaped with the aid of tools. Slip and oxide decorations embellished the pieces. The surface was then polished and compressed with pebbles before firing. In the 16th century the Spanish conquerors discovered not only elaborate gold work, but also high-quality advanced ceramics. The tribes of North and South America still make pottery in the traditional way. The many different coloured earths of America lend themselves easily to the manufacture of ceramics and to their decoration with bright colours.

Majolica, Faience, Delft

The above are three ceramic painting techniques named after their places of origin (Majolica began on the Spanish Mediterranean island of Majorca; Faience is a town in northern Italy; and Delft is in Holland). The characteristic of these painting techniques consists in applying paint to the unfired glaze with oxides or other materials. Through etching, together with glaze, the decoration is indelibly joined to the pottery, a technique that originated in the near East. Here, glazes were used around 2,000 BC. A totally independent style of Islamic ceramics originated in the 9th century. Initially, there were blue-white decorations which were copied in China, and were the forerunners of the blue-white porcelains. The development of Islamic ceramics occurred through constant exchange with China.

RIGHT: **Faience vase by Rene Buthaud, France, 1925.**

BELOW: **A Minton majolica wine cooler, 1856. Minton developed a range of decorative earthenwares with brightly coloured low-temperature glazes inspired by Italian majolica.**

The most significant independent achievement of Muslim ceramics is the 9th-century gleaming metallic lustre glaze and tiles, usually painted and used as building decoration. Elaborate religious inscriptions appear on the tiles and dishes. Later, this calligraphy developed into ornamentation as arabesques. The potters painted on a pewter glaze with cobalt blue, copper green, yellowish brown (iron oxide) and manganese brown. The most conspicuous element of these ceramics is their brilliant colours, not least since this was a time when simple ceramics were prevalent in Europe.

Across Moorish Spain, Faience linked Eastern and Western cultures. The Crusaders brought tiles to Europe to be used in public baths and palaces, which were also decorated with intricately shaped mosaics. Such was the demand for these items that a significant pottery industry grew up around Malaga and Valencia, the trade centre being Majorca (the term Majolica first appeared in the

gothic family), *famiglia alla porcellane* (showing the Chinese influence), and *stile bello* (beautiful style). Manufacturers sprung up everywhere, painting and working in different ways, creating their own style. After the emphasis on lavish decoration came a period of moderation, limited to blue, yellow, orange and green.

The Dutch were also famous Faience painters, and developed their own style from Italian patterns. Tiles and plates were at first traditionally painted, then Delft later fell increasingly under the Chinese influence.

When Johannes Friedrich Bottger introduced porcelain into Europe in 1708/9, the influence of this fine white ceramic mass could no longer be halted. Faience is admittedly still manufactured in small factories, but they are no longer of economic significance.

MODERN EUROPEAN CERAMICS

In the 18th and 19th centuries potters confined themselves mostly to necessities as they had since Roman times – fine tableware was now made of porcelain. Even small ceramic sculptures, artistically manufactured and shaped, used the new material. Art Nouveau worked with finer materials: glass, silver, pearls and ivory. Only after World War One, due to mass production and industrialization, did a clay renaissance begin. The Bauhaus movement in Weimar and Dessau determined the lines. With cheap mass-produced pottery new clear ceramics came over to Europe. A return to old pottery traditions took place. There were no traces of the richly decorated ware of the 17th and 18th centuries. From this return to the easily-shaped material clay, and the development of glazes arose new types of work.

15th century). From Majorca the goods went to Italy and southern France. In Italy, Majolica production was carried out in the Umbrian area and Tuscany.

Faience is a decorative pattern with architectural decorations, geometrical elements, foliage, weapons, animals, scenes from antiquity, and Old Testament biblical scenes. Soon the artists gained in self-confidence and began signing their works, and families devoted to the art came into being. Vessels and dishes were not merely signed, but also decorated with half-reliefs. Lucca della Robbia developed large sculptures using this technique. New stylistic methods also developed including *stile severo* (the severe style), *famiglia verde* (the green family), *famiglia florale gotica* (floral

CHAPTER *one*

◆·◆·◆·◆·◆·◆·◆

Ceramics Earth, Water, Air and Fire

LEFT: **A blue-veined Raku pot by Harvey Sadow Jr, USA. The blue colour is given by copper oxide.**

Earth

◆ ⸱ ⸱ ◆ ⸱ ⸱ ◆ ⸱ ⸱ ◆ ⸱ ⸱ ◆ ⸱ ⸱ ◆ ⸱ ⸱ ◆

The key ingredient for pottery is clay. Clays are continuously being formed by the decomposition of feldspar-rich rocks. The melting rivers of the Ice Age created the great clay beds. These immense rivers carried great lumps of rock which broke down into small pieces, which in turn were carried further afield by the water. When the rivers slowed on the fluvial plains and in the valleys, small particles of clay were deposited. Over the centuries these deposits increased to sizeable depths. Other clay beds were produced by the weathering action of wind, frost, water and heat. In addition, plants shooting up through the earth set the decomposition process in motion.

The resultant clay is a fine, sedimentary rock of grey, green, yellow, red, or blue colour. The colour of the earth depends on the origin of the rock, and its dominant minerals. Clays often also contain quartz and mica. In places where aluminium oxide minerals occur in their purest form, kaolin is produced, a prerequisite for porcelain manufacture. Although nature is still producing clay, the ready-made kind is best for pottery. You are guaranteed better results.

The ancient potters laid down great clay beds, which were exposed to the weather, cleaned, and kneaded – a lengthy procedure. It is alleged that Japanese potters prepared clay for their descendants in this way. In fact it is still done in small workshops today. Fortunately our clays are now specially prepared from clay paste, fireclay, and water – a far more reliable mix.

It is also worth noting that potters work mostly with clay that is appropriate for turning pots but which is not always suitable for other techniques. And, although coarse clay is available from

ABOVE RIGHT: **A Japanese Bizen pot which uses a local clay from one of the many pottery districts of Japan. The pots are wound in twisted rice straw to give the particular colour effect.**

BELOW RIGHT: **Clay bodies are normally categorized according to their firing temperature. In this picture are seen (from top) red clay, the most common, and used in earthenware; bone China clay, mainly used for casting; stoneware and white earthenware clay, two grey varieties that are hard to distinguish; porcelain clay, the whitest of prepared bodies after firing; and black clay, prepared by mixing red clay with a black stain.**

brickworks, it is rarely workable and cannot be used for fine pieces.

Before buying clay, consideration must be given to several matters. First, clays are available in various colours: white, yellow, red, brown and black. These tones have no influence on plasticity or stability, but come from the addition of oxides. If you want to produce a light-coloured item, use a light-coloured clay, and so on. However, note that a beige mixture becomes red

through chemical change during firing.

Today, the industrial manufacture of consistent clay mixtures of the highest quality, for a multitude of applications, is possible. They are used for a variety of purposes – in electrical engineering (for insulation); in space technology; in modern cookers (made from glass ceramics); huge sewage pipes (ceramic), and micro-chips (also ceramic). And, since ceramics are bio-compatible, they are of benefit to doctors performing hip replacements and dentists, who have been working with ceramics for a long time.

For our purposes we need only distinguish between lean and fat clays. We have already discussed the lean clay, which potters need for throwing. Now we come to the fat mixture which contains little fireclay. Fireclay consists of fired, crushed clay particles, but we will not use it for throwing on the wheel (although many potters can and do), because our hands would be cut by the sharp edges. During drying the volume decreases and cracks quickly develop. However, in pieces which have been thrown, the danger of crack formation is not so great, because the pieces are round and can shrink evenly. From the damp clay to the fired piece, shrinkage amounts to around 10 per cent, and up to 50 per cent in special mixtures. The coarse or lean clay contains a proportion of fireclay causing a decrease in plasticity, but it is more stable and the drying process is less problematic. The advantage of fireclay is that during firing it holds its shape well although the shard is coarser and more porous.

The problem so far has been finding a good material. But do not worry, clay can easily be mixed, and different mixtures are available. Coarse clays contain

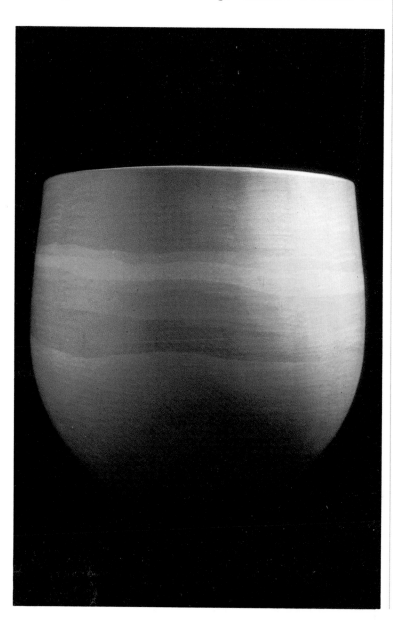

BELOW: **Coiled and burnished pot by Ann Harris, UK, demonstrating a subtle and attractive use of three coloured clays – chocolate, red and orange.**

many large grains of fireclay for large, thick pieces, such as slabs and pot lids. There are also mixtures with less coarse grains for figures or large vases. Fine-grain mixtures, with a low proportion of fireclay, are used to make fine figures, brooches and beads, or for decorating larger pieces. Another option is throwing clay which has a very low proportion of very fine fireclay. And finally there is medium-grain fireclay, used in sculpture.

To be certain of buying the right kind, do seek advice. You will find that clay is mostly weighed in 10kg (22lb) or 25kg (55lb) pieces and wrapped in plastic covers. Clay which is stored in an airtight container can be kept as long as you wish. If it should dry out, break up the hard lumps into pieces, place them in a covered bucket of water, and leave overnight. The next morning excess water can be poured away or soaked up with a sponge. What is left in the bucket is a clay sludge, which must be spread out on plaster boards. Wait until most of the water has been soaked up by the plaster and then knead the clay. It is now ready to be used (but throw away dirty clay).

ABOVE: **Premier French ceramics designer Rene Buthaud created this stoneware vase, with its exotic Negro figure, in the 1930s.**

Water

◆ ‥ ◆ ‥ ◆ ‥ ◆ ‥ ◆ ‥ ◆ ‥ ◆

Clay contains not only water, but also chemically bound water which vaporizes during firing. Think of clay minerals as small chips layered one above the other. These chips are surrounded by water which lubricates, making the clay workable. The more minerals clay has, the more plastic it is, and the more water it contains. During firing the interstratal water evaporates, which means that clay pieces slightly reduce in size. Interstratal and chemically bound

water is responsible for this effect. Finally, note the danger from water which turns into steam. If an item of pottery is not sufficiently dried, steam bursts out and shatters it.

Air

◆ ‥ ◆ ‥ ◆ ‥ ◆ ‥ ◆ ‥ ◆ ‥ ◆

The greater the shrinkage, during drying, the wetter the clay would have been. Shrinkage during drying for pieces with an average fireclay content amounts to approximately 5–8 per cent. The fatter (and wetter) the clay, the greater the shrinkage. Pieces can therefore easily lose their shape, and even crack through uneven drying. Draughts must obviously be avoided, as must drying too quickly. In tall pieces the water can sink to the bottom, with vases losing their proportion as they shrink noticeably higher up. As tensions occur the vase will inevitably crack. The situation is similar with dishes and large plates – the edge dries more quickly than the centre and cracks form.

One solution involves placing items on an absorbent material, such as plaster boards or newspaper. Boards with holes are also suitable allowing the water to drain away, but avoid placing pieces in a draught. Dry slowly, covering each individual part. Over a tall vase place a plastic sheet which is raised slightly every day so the vase can dry slowly from the bottom to the top. However, it is very difficult to dry bowls and plates evenly. For the best results place them on an absorbent material and change their position occasionally, so that they do not stand in water. Cover them to dry very slowly in a cool place. High-edged dishes can be wrapped, but do take care not to break them.

The pieces can be kept safe on drying shelves and in drying cupboards. When drying cracks occur, they can be repaired if spotted at an early stage; if left too long, the damage will be beyond repair. It is therefore best to carry out occasional checks. When the pieces are completely dry, handle them gently. Never carry a vessel by the handle and hold each piece with two hands. Incidentally, it is better to leave a piece drying slightly longer, than to place it in the kiln whilst still damp, leading to steam damage.

Fire

Within the firing temperature range of 180–250°C (356–482°F), water vaporizes. Yet despite the firing, the pieces will not be completely dry – there is still water trapped in the walls or the base. Air pockets can also cause problems. As the hot air expands it is unable to escape slowly through the glaze, and bursts out, destroying the work. To avoid such problems heat the kiln slowly.

Between 450–600°C (842–1,112°F) the chemically combined water escapes, the silica crystals change, and clay earth becomes ceramic. This means that heat should be applied more slowly so that pieces of pottery survive this firing phase intact; thereafter you can fire without interruption up to 900–940°C (1,652–1,724°F). At this temperature the pottery is hard and so porous that the glaze will hold. Leave it to cool slowly and be patient. However, if you wish to apply a glaze, the vase must go into the fire again, for the glost or glaze firing. The temperature is now increased to 1,000–1,300°C (1,832–2,372°F) depending on whether you are making earthenware, stoneware, or porcelain. This firing stage expels the last few traces of water and the works expand and contract. The glaze is now joined inextricably to the pot. Just as we had to be patient during the initial biscuit firing and were unable to remove the pieces from the fire before sufficient cooling had occurred, we must wait for the glaze to cool. For those who are patient there should be no problems.

ABOVE: **This porcelain flock was designed by sculptor Edouard-Marcel Sandoz in the late 1920s.**

LEFT: **The British pottery Carter, Stabler and Adams made this colourful earthenware vase. All of their pots were hand-thrown and hand-decorated.**

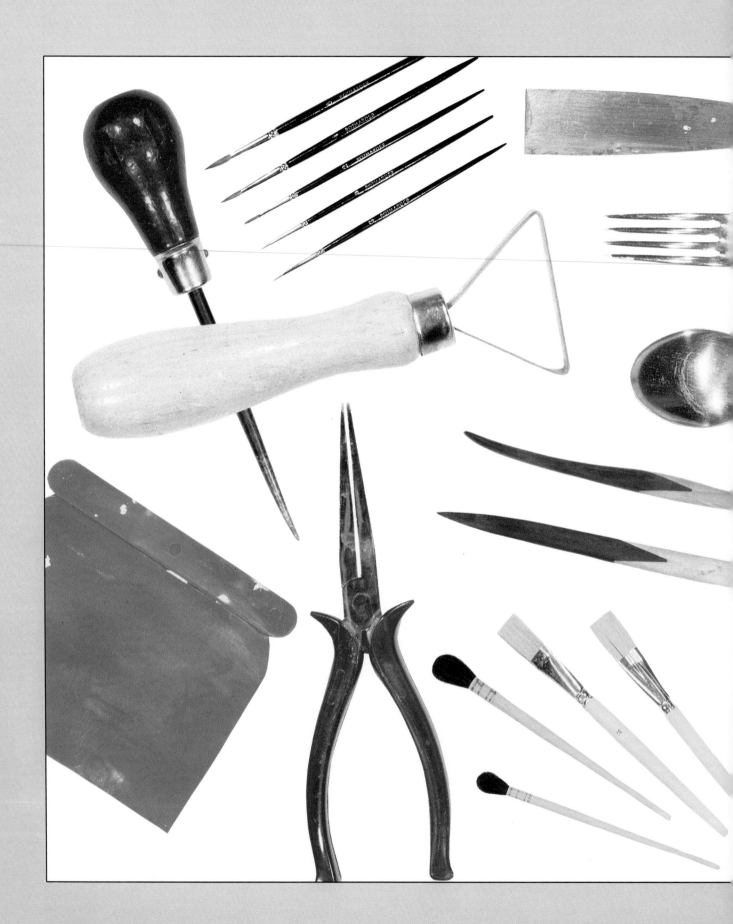

CHAPTER *two*

◆·······◆·······◆·······◆·······◆

Equipment

LEFT: **Some of the equipment you will need before making pottery.**

For the simplest clay shapes you need little equipment, just an absorbent cloth, a small wooden board, cutting wire and a small knife. If you want to economize use a wooden kitchen board and a cooking knife. A cut-up sheet will provide the cloth. Proper hand tools are essential. When buying tools always look for quality and effectiveness.

To begin with, work with clay in a fairly basic way to provide a chance to experience the material, feel how long it remains malleable, when it becomes dry, and when it starts to crack. Clay rewards careful handling, and does not like to be worked for too long – it can crumble to pieces.

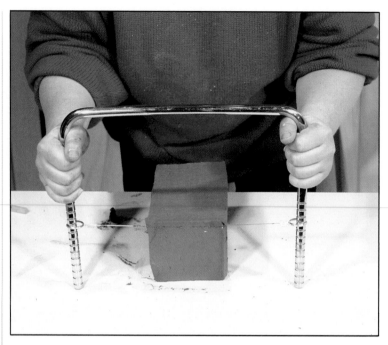

The work table should be stable, with a hard waterproof board. An oilcloth cover with a smooth surface is quite safe; the sharp fireclay edges, which can leave scratches on polished wood, will not cut this surface. In case this still seems too risky, work the clay on a board. Under the clay lay the cloth which prevents the clay from sticking to the surface. When you finish a piece place the finished work on a small board, preferably wooden. Again, place a cloth between the two surfaces, partly to soak up excess water.

First, however, cut the clay from the block with the wire. For shaping, smoothing and cutting, use the kitchen knife.

The next stage involves using a potter's wheel, enabling you to turn a piece and work on it from all sides. Accomplished handymen can even make their own wheels. Shops, however, offer a choice of wheels made from steel, cast steel, and aluminium; those with ball-bearings run smoothest. Wheels available for purchase have a diameter of 20–30cm (6.7–10in). You can buy wheels without a tripod which are placed on tables (table wheels) these are sufficient for school and home use. Their advantage is that after use they can be put away in a cupboard or on the shelf. Wheels with tripods are height-adjustable and stand free. Again, a cloth placed between the work and the wheel means you can detach the work more easily. For drying pieces of pottery use plaster boards, which soak up excess water. They are preferable to wooden boards.

ABOVE: **Showing the correct way to use the cutting wire on a piece of clay.**

LEFT: **Sieve and bowl, needed for sieving the glaze.**

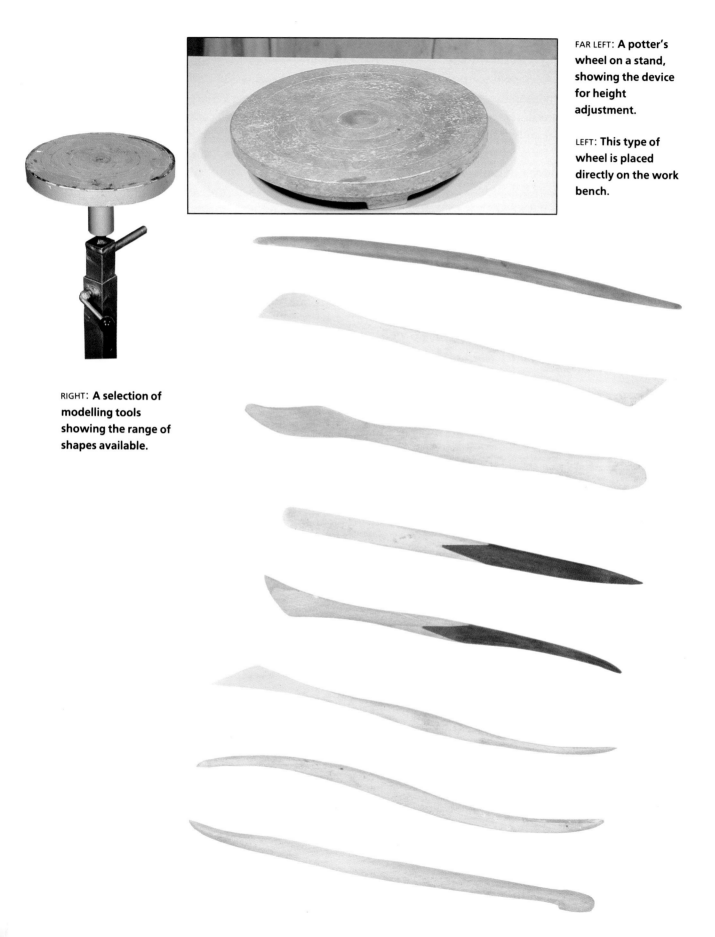

FAR LEFT: **A potter's wheel on a stand, showing the device for height adjustment.**

LEFT: **This type of wheel is placed directly on the work bench.**

RIGHT: **A selection of modelling tools showing the range of shapes available.**

After your initial attempts at pottery, it will be clear that tools besides your hands are necessary. A modelling tool has two differently-shaped ends. Depending on your needs, select a tool providing a long spoon and edges for a variety of purposes, from cutting to smoothing. Good modelling tools are made from wood, usually box or ebony. The harder the wood, the easier it is to work with. There are also simple plastic designs, but these soon become insufficient for your needs (for kindergartens and schools where high turnover must be reckoned with, these simple designs will suffice). Various pottery knives are also available, although a broad palette knife is best. Otherwise, a kitchen knife will suffice. However, modelling tools and mirettes are still very important. (You should purchase at least three mirettes and a variety of modelling tools.) That many are needed for shaping, removing clay from the work, and hollowing out thick pieces. Where modelling tools are too coarse, use sharper tools. With these you can carve out particularly delicate shapes, and carve your initials and the date of manufacture on the base. Alternative tools are knitting needles and toothpicks. If you want to make round holes for hanging pieces, or for patterns, try buying hole cutters. Alternatively, use an apple-corer. Forks are also extremely useful devices for roughening, engraving and scratching patterns. For smoothing and thickening use a beater, though always with the greatest care lest you knock a piece of pottery out of shape.

For shaping and preparing slabs of clay you need a clay roller. There are

BELOW: **You will need at least one knife; a kitchen knife is quite adequate. A cloth and wooden sticks for modelling are also important.**

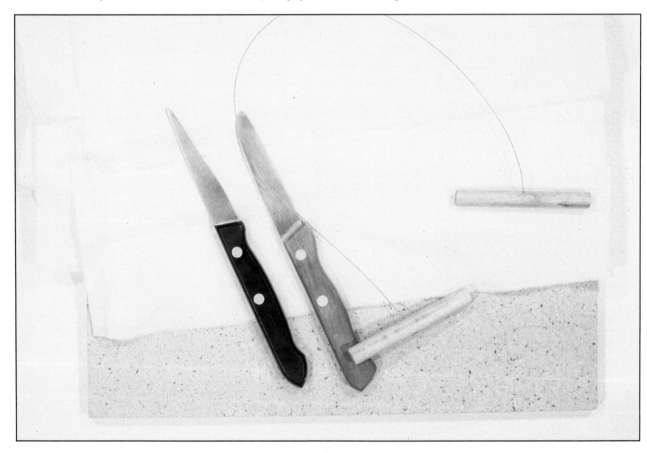

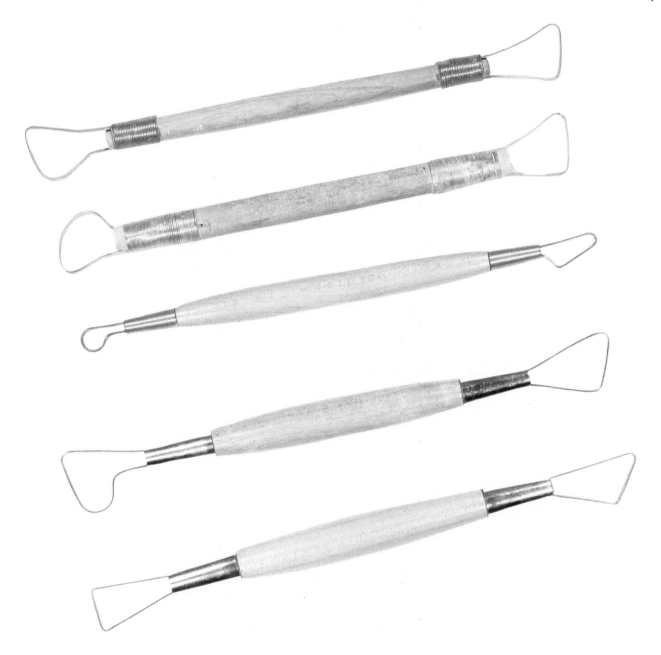

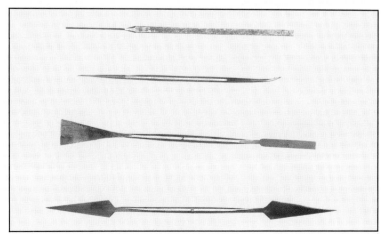

ABOVE: **Different sized mirettes are handy for working with varied pieces of pottery.**

LEFT: **Sharp metal tools to be used for carving patterns or lettering.**

ABOVE: **A broad-handled cutting wire for carving out larger forms.**

BELOW: **You will need a mortar and pestle for grinding glazes.**

two kinds — a roller with ball-bearings (rolling pin), or a simple round stick with a diameter of about 35mm (1.4in). To create slabs of equal strength, work in two directions. And to obtain even, thick slabs, cut them with the cutting bow from the mass of clay.

When using the technique called turning, further aids are required, such as turning guides and sponges. Turning guides are similar to modelling tools, being made from hard wood, though some are plastic or metal; see which suits you best. Also necessary while turning are a small bucket of water and a sponge to soak up excess moisture. Natural sponges are preferable, being softer and more pliable than artificial sponges, but they are also more expensive. A sponge on a stick is useful for tall vessels.

Glazing aids

ABOVE: **Two types of rollers – choose either a rolling pin or a round stick.**

◆ ⋯ ◆ ⋯ ◆ ⋯ ◆ ⋯ ◆ ⋯ ◆ ⋯ ◆

A well glazed work is aesthetically pleasing; a badly glazed work can ruin an otherwise professionally made item. Here again, appropriate tools are the key to success. For glazing, various flat bristle brushes are available – but do not economize. Glazing brushes are 20–75mm (0.8–3in) wide. For most surfaces, a brush with a width of 25mm (1in) will suffice. Purchase a different brush for each glaze required to avoid rinsing after each session. When decorating finished pieces that have overglaze, middle glaze, and underglaze, you need fine to very fine animal-hair paintbrushes. Initially basic brushes will suffice, but for the best results you need

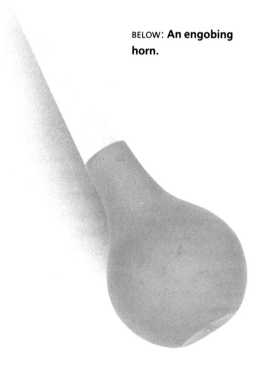

BELOW: **An engobing horn.**

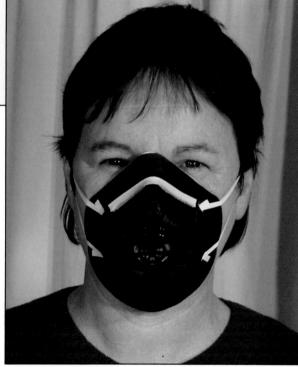

ABOVE: **Various pieces of equipment: a needle for removing air pockets; templates for accurate shaping; cutting wire to turn pieces off the wheel; and a basin and sponge.**

RIGHT: **A dust mask such as this is vital protection against fumes.**

more expensive brushes. You can apply engobe with the engobing horn.

Initial attempts to apply the glaze can be made by spraying with a standard glaze spray. If however you wish to spray regularly, spraying equipment with an extractor unit must be purchased. In order to apply the glazes, use a glazing sieve. And finally, when mixing glazes, raw materials and engobes, always wear a dust mask to protect the mouth, since glazes contain unpleasant and often poisonous gases.

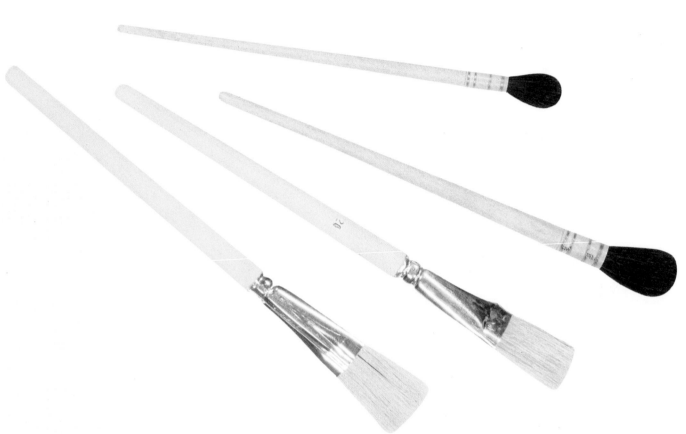

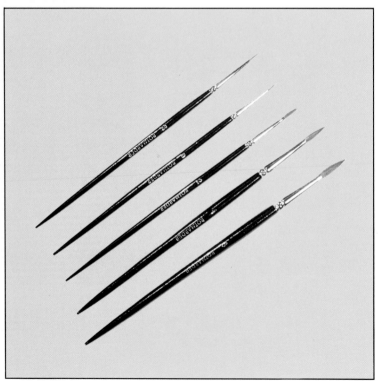

ABOVE: **Don't stint on buying good brushes, such as these glazing brushes.**

LEFT: **Very fine natural hair brushes are needed to decorate finished pieces.**

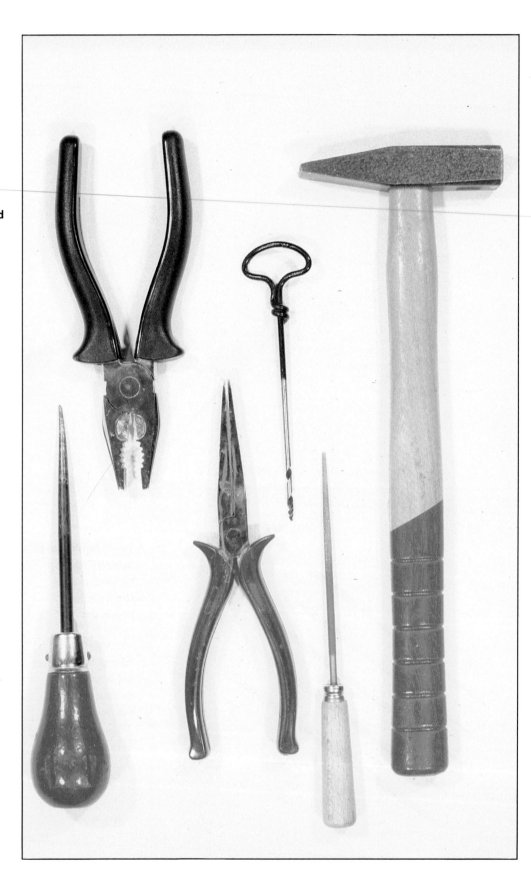

RIGHT: **Some of the smaller pieces of equipment that every workshop should have, including hammer, pliers, drill and round file.**

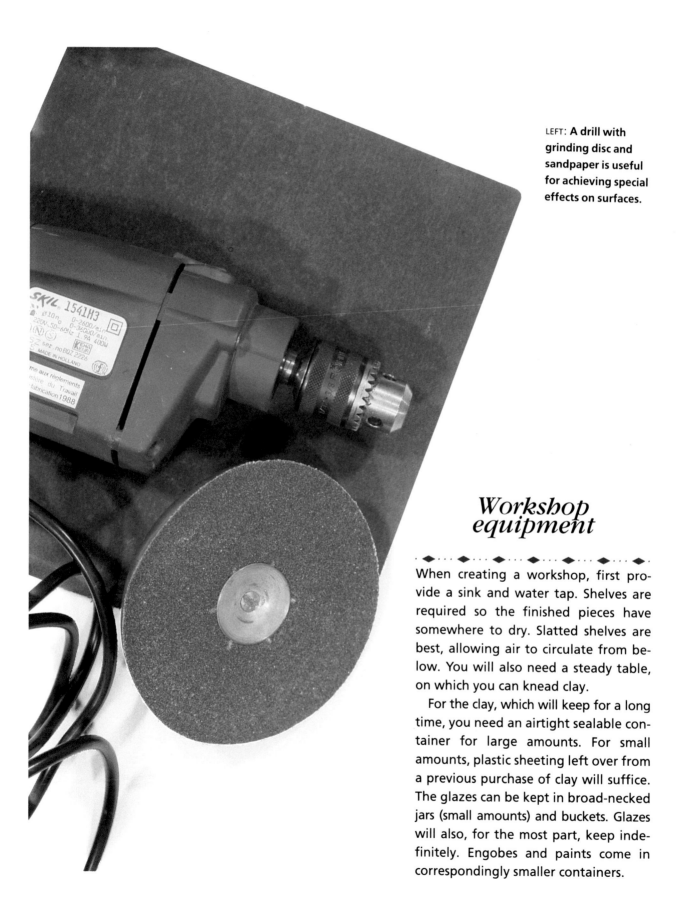

LEFT: **A drill with grinding disc and sandpaper is useful for achieving special effects on surfaces.**

Workshop equipment

When creating a workshop, first provide a sink and water tap. Shelves are required so the finished pieces have somewhere to dry. Slatted shelves are best, allowing air to circulate from below. You will also need a steady table, on which you can knead clay.

For the clay, which will keep for a long time, you need an airtight sealable container for large amounts. For small amounts, plastic sheeting left over from a previous purchase of clay will suffice. The glazes can be kept in broad-necked jars (small amounts) and buckets. Glazes will also, for the most part, keep indefinitely. Engobes and paints come in correspondingly smaller containers.

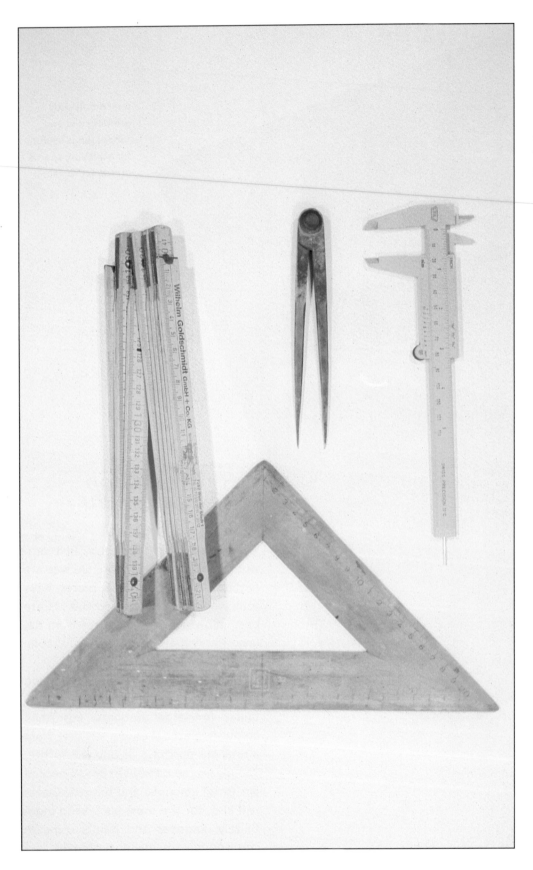

LEFT: **A compass, set
square and slide
gauge will allow you
to achieve a
professional finish.**

ABOVE: **Simple tools such as kitchen forks, spatulas and spoons are handy for smoothing and decorating.**

Smaller pieces of equipment include a long ruler, a hammer and chisel, sandpaper, and possibly a grinding wheel, as well as drills, pliers and screwdrivers. Even dividers sometimes come in handy.

Potter's wheels and kilns are larger purchases and require careful consideration. For both, seek the advice of specialist shops. There are foot-driven or electric-powered potter's wheels. Electric table-top wheels are also available on which you can turn small pieces.

In the case of kilns there are various electric versions that are not too large. Gas kilns can be heated with propane gas and have many uses (including reduction firing), although previous experience is necessary when using them. Note that there must be a means of removing waste gases. For both types of kiln there are fireclay bats, kiln props and small tripods or strips on which pots are placed for firing. You will also need gloves for handling warm pots.

Before glaze firing, coat fireclay bats with a special wash to prevent running glaze sticking to the expensive bats. However, if you cannot afford, or do not wish to buy a kiln, you can usually use such facilities at a local club.

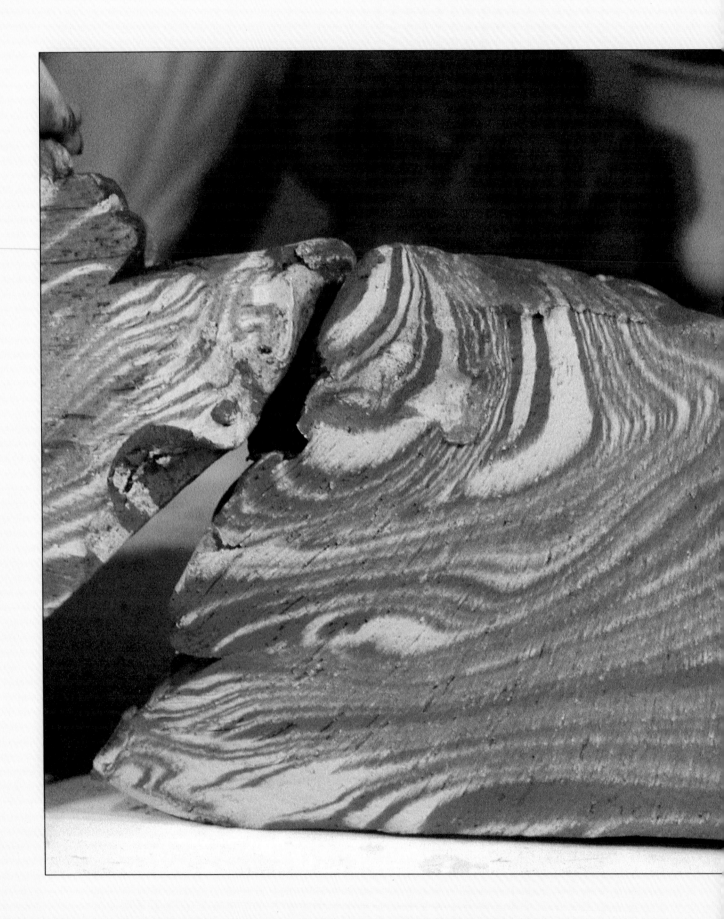

CHAPTER *three*

◆•◆•◆•◆•◆•◆•◆

Moulding with Clay

LEFT: **Two pieces of different-coloured clay are worked together to demonstrate the number of layers achieved by kneading.**

First steps

◆ ⋯ ◆ ⋯ ◆ ⋯ ◆ ⋯ ◆ ⋯ ◆ ⋯ ◆

The essential techniques for working clay are kneading and applying the slip. Kneading the clay is every bit as crucial as selecting the right type of clay. Before buying the clay it will have been through mixing machines and factory extruders. It is marketed in hanks and packaged in plastic covers. These packages of clay usually weigh either 10kg (22lb) or 25kg (55lb).

Although the clay has been well prepared, cleaned and mixed, it still requires kneading. The purpose of kneading is to spread the clay minerals, which are in the shape of small tiles, throughout the material, giving it a regular internal structure. Such kneading can only be carried out when the clay is first mixed with fireclay and water.

Kneading cannot be avoided. Its prime functions also include making the clay more plastic and malleable; it expels air bubbles, too, which will exist even in specially bought material. These air bubbles can have a devastating effect during firing. They expand at high temperatures and can easily shatter a piece if they cannot escape through the

porous shard. Another potential problem can occur during wheel turning. Centrifugal force can propel air bubbles to the outside, ruining the pot's shape.

Before kneading, take a large piece of clay, weighing approximately 10kg (22lb). Place it on a steady table or hard surface. Place the cutting wire under the centre of the clay, and pull upwards, giving two pieces of equal size. Place one on top of the other and begin to knead. Next, turn the clay in a quarter circle to the left, and repeat the process. Again, use the wire to cut the clay

through the middle from below. Both lumps of clay are again kneaded one on top of the other, giving a piece with four layers. After the next operation there are eight layers, and by the time this has been done 20 times the clay is a well processed malleable mass.

There is another, slightly less arduous way of preparing the clay. This technique can however, only be used on small amounts. Cut a manageable 1–2kg (2.2–4.4lb) piece of clay from the lump, knead it on the table, and turn the clay in on itself like a snail-shell. It is important to work in only one direction, not forcing in any extra air bubbles.

1 Cutting the piece of clay in half with the cutting wire.

2 Two pieces of different-coloured clay ready for kneading.

3 Kneading, the clay by turning it in on itself.

4 After kneading, the clay is shaped into a smooth ball.

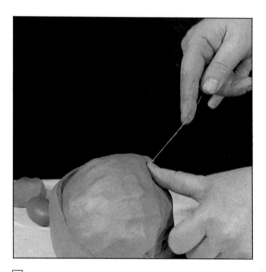

5 Cutting the correct sized piece of clay to be used.

6 Only work on as much clay as you think you will need for each piece.

Slip

◆ · · · ◆ · · · ◆ · · · ◆ · · · ◆ · · · ◆ · · · ◆

The slip is fine clay washed with a lot of water. Such sticky clay is required when attaching clay strips, creating tiles, or making repairs.

While you work the clay, you will find that small crumbs of clay result which dry very quickly. Collect them in a sealable jar and cover with water. After a couple of hours these dry remains will become a soft clay paste, or slip. Always keep the jar sealed for a ready supply. New crumbs can be added to it and again covered with water. To offset evaporation, top up with water from time to time. The slip should always have the consistency of paste, not liquid.

Clay slip can easily be combined with any work. The shaped pieces which are to be joined together are grazed with a fork, coated with slip, and joined together with gentle pressure. Slabs for joining together are cut with a rough edge – then apply plenty of slip to the joins and attach. For a really tight join insert a thin strip of clay into the connections. The slip penetrates the roughened and incised parts of the work and becomes inextricably linked with it. Any superfluous slip on the joins is left to dry and is removed with a scraper or knife. If it is removed too soon you run the risk of damaging the work irreparably.

Two pieces can never be joined together without a slip connection. Shortcuts never work and result in disasters during firing.

From clay to pottery

The following procedure is standard. Practise it again and again until it is second nature. It is impossible to proceed without having mastered these stages.

☐1 Clay kneading (see explanation at the beginning of this chapter).

☐2 Removing the required amount of clay and shaping it into a ball.

☐3 Forming the piece.

☐4 If decorations are to be applied, do this now. Provided the clay is still soft you can incise, stamp, impress, and attach pieces to it.

☐5 Hollowing out – if a piece is more than 2cm (0.8in) thick, it must be hollowed out to remove trapped air bubbles. For hollowing out, slice the piece in two with the cutting wire. Before cutting, remember to mark a spot on the cutting line so that the pieces can be fitted exactly together.

The clay is carefully hollowed out from the inside with a scraper. The thickness of the remaining wall is approximately 4–10mm (0.16–0.4in) according to the piece. Stick it back together with slip and make a small open-

ABOVE: **Slipware cockerel dish by William Newland, UK. The white slip was applied to the red body and the design then trailed with a warm, dark clay.**

BELOW: **A porcelain incised dish by Ann Clark, UK. The design was incised into the clay body at the leather-hard stage. When biscuited, it was glazed with a transparent glaze then fired to 2,340°F (1,280°C).**

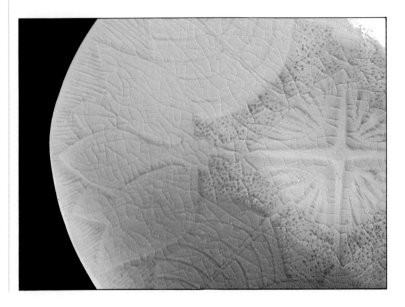

RIGHT: **Showing how pigments react with glazes. Six basic colouring oxides were added to a standard transparent alkaline glaze and a standard transparent lead-based glaze.**

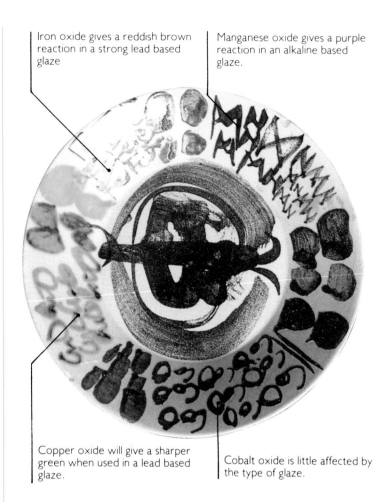

Iron oxide gives a reddish brown reaction in a strong lead based glaze

Manganese oxide gives a purple reaction in an alkaline based glaze.

Copper oxide will give a sharper green when used in a lead based glaze.

Cobalt oxide is little affected by the type of glaze.

ing so that the expanding air can escape.

6 Now is the time to paint the work. Do it when the clay has become leather-hard.

7 Carefully place the work on a shelf to dry. The clay becomes brittle, and dries out, so special care is necessary. From now on handle any item with both hands. Never attempt to lift the work by its attached parts or handle. These parts are extremely delicate and break off immediately. Damage to pieces which are already dry are almost beyond repair. (The drying process is described in detail on page 20.)

8 Biscuit firing. Once the pieces are well dried, they are carefully placed in the kiln and exposed to the fire. After the kiln has cooled down, remove the pieces. Although they are no longer as delicate as before firing, do not pick them up by pieces which could easily break off. Methods of firing and placing pieces in the kiln are described in detail in chapter 9.

9 The work is glazed and painted. You will learn more about these techniques in chapter 8.

10 Glost firing. After this stage the finished pieces can be removed from the kiln. If drops of glaze are hanging on the base, sand them on the grinding wheel or with sandpaper. Care must be taken because splinters of glaze are sharp.

CHAPTER *four*
❖ ﹒ ❖ ﹒ ❖ ﹒ ❖ ﹒ ❖ ﹒ ❖ ﹒ ❖ ﹒ ❖ ﹒

Pottery without a Wheel

LEFT: **These dolls are not as difficult to make as they look – see page 52 for instructions.**

Hand building and pinch pots

Having mastered the introductory stages, it is time to discuss the basic 'creative' techniques. The first, for making a small dish, merely involves squeezing and shaping the ball of clay. This pinching technique requires only your hands and a cutting wire for removing the clay. Use standard, semi-plastic clay. For decorating you will also need a brush. Since you are using only your hands, you can work quickly. As the hands become warm they quickly dry the clay, making it crack. It is therefore advisable to have a slightly damp sponge on the table to wet your hands.

1 From the kneaded clay, cut a fist-sized piece and shape it into a ball.

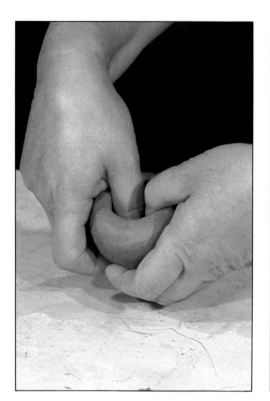

2 With the thumb of one hand make a depression in the clay while pressing lightly against the inside with the other hand. Rotate the ball at the same time.

3 The walls become thinner and are pushed upwards. Take care to work from bottom to top; if you work the edge first, it cracks and becomes limp.

4 To form the edge, run lightly over it with your fingertips. With one hand keep the edge in shape and with the other, carefully smooth it.

5 The outside surface of the pot is smoothed with a modelling stick.

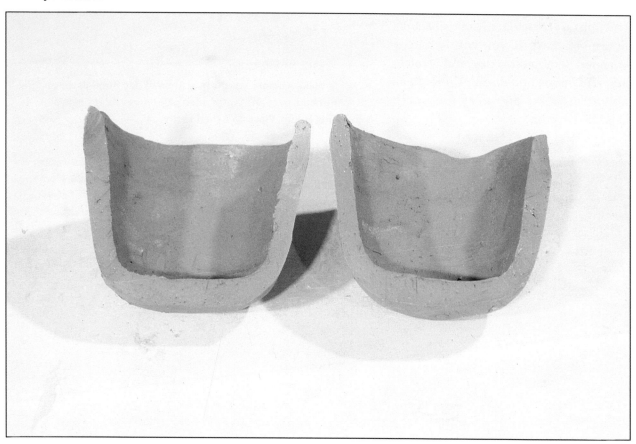

6 A cross-section showing the finished form of your pinch pot.

Hand flatterer

◆ · · · ◆ · · · ◆ · · · ◆ · · · ◆ · · · ◆ · · · ◆

For the second piece of work, a hand flatterer, again you need only use your hands. This time, however, use clay containing fine fireclay. Take a piece large enough to fit inside the hand. Squeeze the clay into shape, letting it follow the shape of your hand. Next, let it dry, polish it with your palms and fingertips, and place it to dry on the shelf next to the dishes. If the dish was a rather useful object, the hand flatterer is certainly not. It has aesthetic rather than practical value.

Small figurative animals

◆ · · · ◆ · · · ◆ · · · ◆ · · · ◆ · · · ◆ · · · ◆

The third piece of work is a small animal figure. To make it you will require a kneaded semi-plastic clay and scratching and modelling tools. These small figurative works are great fun, much liked by children.

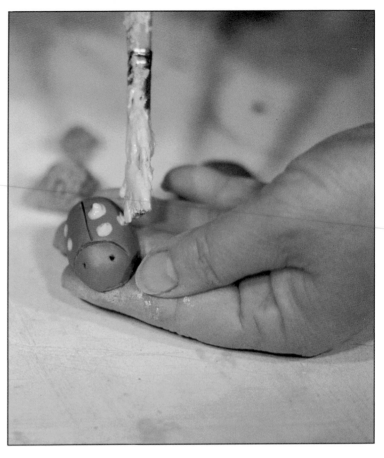

ABOVE: **To make a beetle, cut the oval lump of clay through the middle. Carve the head, eyes and wings, then paint on spots of slip in a contrasting colour. Place on a shelf to dry.**

LEFT: **Little animals are made from small pieces of clay formed in oval shapes.**

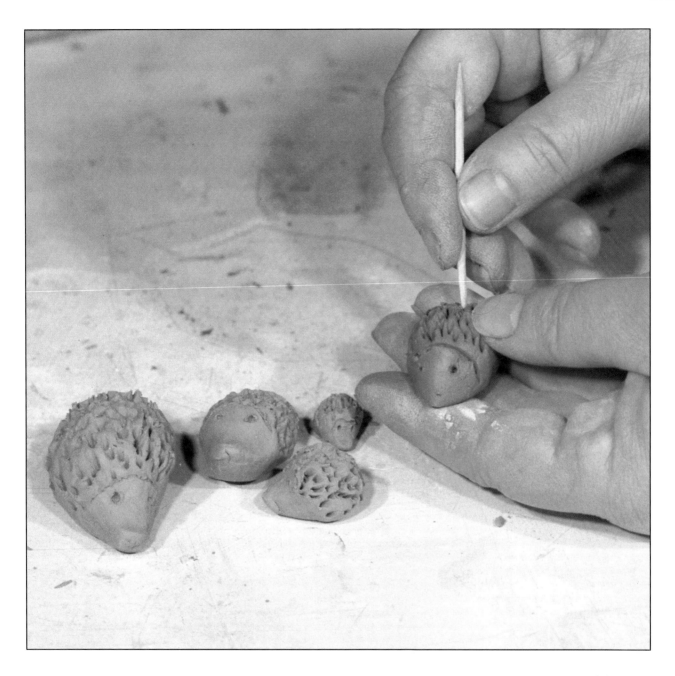

ABOVE: **For a small hedgehog, squeeze a little nose. The spines are created by piercing the clay with scissors. Alternatively, make them separately and attach with slip. The eyes and mouth are carved in.**

For the small *bird* you will need slightly more time. The head comes from a second, slightly smaller oval ball of clay. Attach this with slip to the other piece, to form the bird's body. Now, squeeze the beak out of the lump (a separate beak would break off too easily). Likewise, shape the tail from the lump. However, you can form the feathers and wings from small coils of clay. All the

features – head, eyes, beak and feathers – can be applied by 'scratching' them on. If you have made a large bird with ruffled feathers, pierce it repeatedly from below. This is important so that possible trapped air bubbles do not destroy the work during firing. Using the techniques described, it is possible to create a wide range of animals, and more fantastic creatures.

Jar and lid

◆ ⋯ ◆ ⋯ ◆ ⋯ ◆ ⋯ ◆ ⋯ ◆ ⋯ ◆

The fourth piece of work is a small jar
with lid to contain coins, jewellery, and
small utensils. The material to be used is
once again semi-plastic kneaded clay,
and the tools are cutting wire, a mirette,
and various modelling sticks.

1 **With the cutting
wire remove enough
clay to form a ball
about 7–10 cm (2.7–
4 in) in diameter.
Work the ball of clay
until well rounded;
smooth with a
teaspoon.**

2 **Now place the
cutting wire in the
upper half – hold in
at one end and pull
through until you
have almost split the
clay in two. By
moving the wire
down a little a 'nose'
is created.**

3 The ball is then split into two pieces which fit on top of each other.

4 Take the mirette and slowly start to hollow out the ball with circular motions.

5 Continue the process until the half-ball has a uniformly thick wall, no wider than a little finger.

6 Repeat the process with the other half-ball of clay.

7 Smooth the inner walls with a finger tip.

8 With care, you will find that the two halves will fit exactly on top of each other. Now even the base.

9 To create a small knob for the lid, use a fork to roughen the spot on the lid where the knob will be placed. Do the same to the underside of the ball.

10 Coat both roughened spots with slip and attach the knob. Place the jar on a shelf to dry; insert a sheet of tissue between jar and lid so they don't stick together.

Doll

◆ · · · ◆ · · · ◆ · · · ◆ · · · ◆ · · · ◆ · · · ◆

To make a small doll you need modelling
tools, mirettes, and engraving and knitting needles. The material is semi-plastic
clay. Begin by making the torso and the
head, which are made from one piece.

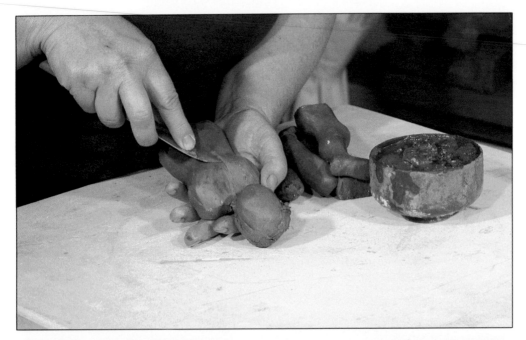

1 Roll the clay into a
cylinder whose
length determines
the size of the figure.
Flatten the cylinder
slightly, and mark
the size of the head.
The legs will take up
approximately half
the body size.

2 Next, shape the
neck – but not too
thinly since it could
easily break; model
the back, shoulders
and chest. The figure
should also have a
waist. Do not forget
to add the chin and
eye sockets. Use a
modelling stick to
work on the hair-
line. If the head
snaps off it can be
reapplied with slip,
but only clean the
join when all other
work is finished.

3 With cutting wire, split the doll's body in half lengthwise.

4 Hollow the doll's body out with a mirette until the edge is approximately 4mm (0.1 in) thick. With practice you should be able to hollow out the head too.

5 Stick the halves together with slip and leave to dry on the shelf.

6 When the slip is dry, clean the join. The air which has been trapped inside must be able to escape during firing, so pierce a small hole as a flue, perhaps at the navel. After firing, apply paint.

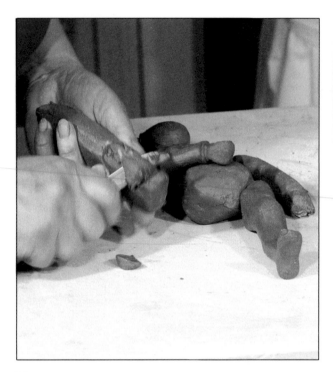

7 To make the arms and legs you need four tubes of clay. Note that a thumb in the right proportions looks better than five fingers sticking out in all directions.

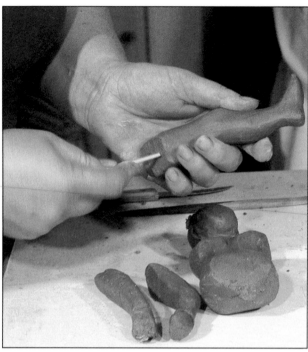

8 If you wish to make a moving doll, pierce holes at the base of the arms and legs, as well as at the elbow joints and thighs.

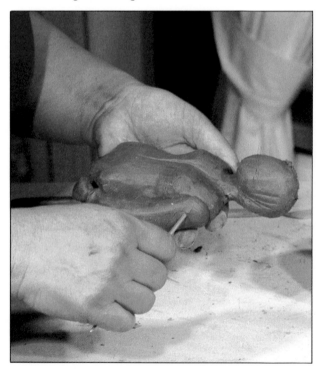

9 After firing insert a thin piece of wire or pass a piece of elastic through these holes to make a moving doll.

1 For a different sort of doll, take two equal lengths of clay. Lay them side by side and form the arms, legs and body from these.

2 The head and neck are placed above the torso; then neck and body are joined together with slip.

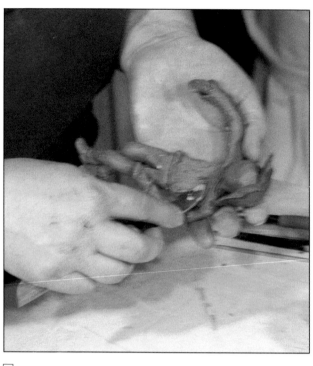

3 Shape and bend the body into a sitting shape with a modelling tool.

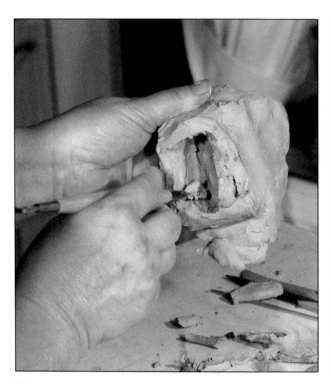

4 If you like, you can make a seat for the figures. Make sure areas thicker than 2cm (0.6 in) are hollowed out.

5 Seat the figures together, creating a natural pose with a modelling tool.

CHAPTER *five*

◆ ━ ◆ ━ ◆ ━ ◆ ━ ◆

The Coiling Technique

LEFT: **Making a vase or mug using the coiling method.**

This technique is probably the most frequently used method when making clay vessels without a potter's wheel. Coils of clay are placed on top of one another. Shapes made from a ball of clay, like a dish, can only be made up to a certain size, after which success becomes difficult, if not impossible. Also, a shape which tapers towards the top, or a closed vessel, are ruled out by this method. However, coiling permits complex structures, and without restriction on size.

Vase or beaker

◆ ⋯ ◆ ⋯ ◆ ⋯ ◆ ⋯ ◆ ⋯ ◆ ⋯ ◆

The first piece of work in this new technique is a vessel (used as a vase, or, if made small, a beaker). The following tools are required: small board or a banding wheel as a base, over which a cloth is placed; modelling tools; small knife for smoothing; and cutting wire. Slip is not normally used with the coiling method as it makes the clay too damp and slippery.

1 Slice off a piece of clay with the cutting wire and roll it into a coil the thickness of a thumb. This provides the base of the vessel and is coiled into a spiral.

2 Do not make the
diameter too large,
or you will end up
with a vessel that is
far too big. It is best
to take an existing
vessel of the right
size and use it as a
guide.

3 With the knife
smooth the base
from top to bottom,
where necessary
cutting it to provide
a round shape. A pair
of dividers will help
establish the shape.
More coils are rolled
out, up to four or five
in total. The first coil
is placed on the edge
of the base and
attached.

4 The first and following coils must be 'welded' to achieve an even shape. If you proceed upwards in one long coil the work loses its shape.

5 Note that you must weld the base and coil inside and outside. Carefully smooth the clay in a downward direction with a modelling tool or your thumb. Once the coil is fixed in position, clean the join in a lateral direction. Put the second coil in place, taking care that the subsequent coil finishes in a different position.

6 & 7 Carefully
smooth the work,
first inside then
outside.

8 As the number of coils increases, it becomes possible to lift the vessel without danger of ruining its shape. From now on the pace of work can increase.

9 Three coils are put in place. All three coils are then smoothed in the same way as before, both inside and outside. Now clean them and continue building to the desired height.

10 & 11 Squeeze the
upper edge between
thumb and
forefinger to make it
thinner, whilst
smoothing it
delicately with the
fingertips of the
other hand.

12

13

If you want to make a vase with a bulbous form, proceed in the following way. At the height where the vase is to become bulbous, place the coils further outwards rather than directly on top of each other. (Be careful: due to pressure whilst smoothing the outside, the clay easily moves out. Hold it in shape with the other hand.) If you now wish to narrow the vessel, attach the coils on the inside and add each coil separately. In this way you can, with some practice, make a spherical vase with a narrow opening.

If the clay becomes too heavy in the upper coils and threatens to break off, fill the vessel with newspaper. Also, whilst working occasionally take a rest so that the clay can dry and become more solid. If you have a large opening, the newspaper can easily be removed after drying. But if there is a small opening, fire the piece with the news-paper inside – it burns without leaving any traces.

Note that the underside of a narrow opening is difficult to smooth and is best done by hand. This enables you to feel the uneven patches and weak points. Whether making a vase or a beaker always take care to create a good rim. And for the final coil take extra care to produce a particularly attractive shape.

If the vessel is not finished on the first day, pack it in a plastic sheet. The more airtight the packing, the longer you can leave it in the plastic, even up to three or four weeks. If for any reason the piece must be packed away for longer, open the package and dampen the piece with a water spray.

Dish or bowl

◆····◆···◆···◆···◆···◆···◆·

For our next piece of work you require the following: a banding wheel; boards; modelling tools and knife.

Note that semi-plastic red firing clay is particularly suitable for this project. And finally, use a kitchen dish or bowl, smooth sided with no narrowing at the top. This will form the mould for the new dish: the inside of the bowl shap-ing the outside of the newly made piece.

First, prepare the bowl so that it can be used as mould, lining it with damp newspaper. Do not use a single piece of newspaper because it will crease and leave traces on the work. Instead tear the newspaper into strips to line the bowl. The lining paper prevents sticking, and ensures the clay can be easily re-moved from the bowl.

Next, use the clay to make the decor-ations – triangles, lozenges, flattened balls, squares, short elongated pieces, and spirals, in fact, whatever shapes you choose. Then roll out the base, as with the preceding vase. Gauge the

LEFT: **Elementary designs are often beautiful in their simplicity yet can be further enhanced by a striking use of colour.**

diameter from the size of the bowl being used as the mould. Place the base into the mould. Coil the first roll and attach it securely. Since you cannot work on the exterior, shape the coils with care. Continue by applying the decorative patterns and smooth the interior with a modelling tool. If you feel the piece is too thin in any place, attach a rolled flat piece of clay with slip and work it well into the wall. For the finishing touch use a coil of clay, a zigzag pattern, or a favourite ornament.

Leave the work to stand in the bowl overnight. By the next morning it will have shrunk and become harder. If you intend using the bowl for fruit, for instance, you will need to reinforce the base. Place it on a ring which has the added advantage of giving the piece extra height. If you wish, you can build one ring on top of another to give a really solid structure.

The base is attached as follows. Remove the bowl from the mould. Carefully place a small soft cushion or several soft cloths inside once it has dried. Ensure the padding is higher than the rim. Place one hand on the cushion and with the other take the mould and turn the bowl. With the opening facing down place it on the wooden board or banding wheel. If possible, the bowl's edges should not come in contact with the board or wheel. The mould can now easily be removed by lifting it upwards. Fortunately, the clay will briefly be sufficiently soft to enable exterior cosmetic repairs to be carried out. If some paper has stuck to the surface, it will be burnt off during firing.

The next stage involves preparing a round coil, preferably shaping it around a can or similar object. Place this coil loose on the base of the bowl, and mark both its inner and outer edge. It is then removed and replaced after you have carved out the area between the marked lines and applied slip. Carefully join the bowl and the base. When the coil is dry, and the bowl can no longer be so easily pulled out of shape, turn the whole piece over and place it on a flat surface, if possible a plaster board. By gently rotating the bowl to and fro, the coil becomes flat, and the bowl stands firm and does not wobble. To dry, stand it on its head – after approximately two days turn it the right way up and remove the cushion or material. After two or three days' further drying the bowl is ready to be placed in the kiln.

Using the same method you can make smooth bowls or dishes, but instead of using decorative clay pieces work with clay coils. As described, remove the work from the mould and, in addition, smooth the exterior. If necessary work with slip, but not if it is too damp, since cracks can easily occur. Apart from this, the smooth bowl is finished as above.

Teapot with lid and tea bowls

◆ · · · ◆ · · · ◆ · · · ◆ · · · ◆ · · · ◆ · · · ◆

The following tools are required: a banding wheel or a small board with a cloth; modelling tools; knife; and knitting needles or toothpicks. Use semi-plastic red firing or black clay. And finally, purchase a cane or bamboo handle from a handicraft shop.

Tea bowls are made in the same way as the vessel using the coiling technique. The one difference is the need for thin coils, no wider than the little finger.

Since the technique has already been described (pages 58–65) it will not be repeated. But note that, as with all drinking vessels, the rim must be thin.

Before constructing the teapot establish the shape – bulbous, straight or even conical. It is best to make a simple drawing, which is easier than you might think, and a cross-section diagram.

Build the pot in the proven way, making the base, attaching the first three coils separately, and smoothing them. Next, add several coils at once. If you are making a large pot, the coils can be quite thick, otherwise keep them thinner. Note that if the sides are too thick, the pot will be very heavy.

If you want a small base on the pot, make it last of all, enabling it to dry.

The teapot's opening requires a hinge or attachment for the lid. If it is to be within the opening, place a thin coil inside as a rest. If the lid sits over the opening, build a small bridge at the edge of the hole. Now turn the pot on its head and fit the base, in the same way as described for making the bowl. Place the pot to one side with the opening facing down.

Roll out the coils, which should be thin. They will form the spout or pourer. Build up the coils, narrowing with height. In the meantime, the base and the pot have hardened to such an extent that the pot can be righted, with the opening at the top. Hold the spout against the pot, and decide where best to attach it. This means one end of the spout will be cut at an angle. Do this carefully, not cutting off too much, since you can take off more later. When satisfied, mark the spot where the spout is to emerge from the pot. Do not attach it too low down because hot water will leak out when you are making tea.

The next stage involves making holes inside the marked surface. Carve along the marked line and apply slip. With gentle, even pressure attach the spout. To be safe, place a thin clay coil around the join and smooth, so disguising minor mistakes which have arisen during cutting. The spout must now be cut off level and shaped by hand. Take care – it can easily come off.

Look down on the pot from above to check the spout is sitting straight. The handle should also lie on this imaginary line opposite the spout.

The teapot *lid* must fit snugly, therefore measure the diameter of the opening on which it sits. If the opening is not round, place tracing paper on the pot and draw a template. Curved slightly upwards, the lid is built with thin coils of clay. Next, make the knob for the lid, which can be plain or decorated. If you have decided on a lid sitting inside the pot, attach a bridge inside. This bridge is made in the same way as the base of the pot and is attached flat. Mark the join on the underside of the lid, remove the bridge, and carve along the marked line, applying slip afterwards. Attach the bridge with light pressure and smooth away the excess slip. The lid is placed carefully on the pot. If it does not fit exactly, the still soft clay can be further worked.

The pot is dried and biscuit fired with the lid on. Through drying and firing together, the two elements will not lose their shape. If the clay is still so damp that there is a danger the two will stick together, place a strip of tissue paper between the pot and the lid. Also note that if the opening is curved, but not round enough for the lid to be turned in the hole, you must make a small cut in the lid and pot.

CHAPTER *six*

❖•••❖•••❖•••❖•••❖

Slab Building

LEFT: **Using a template to cut out decorative shapes.**

Slabs of clay can be made in two different ways: by rolling it out with a clay roller, or by cutting it from a large lump with the aid of a cutting wire. The latter is particularly suitable when you need several slabs of the same length. The clay should form a mass of slabs beaten into a block. The lengths of the sides must have the dimensions of the final slabs. Cut off slabs of equal thickness with the slab cutter.

If you require slabs of varying size, roll out the clay on the cloth, using the roller. If you roll on two battens you obtain a slab of even thickness, from which any shape can be cut. This method of slab building is less strenuous than the other method, but does have disadvantages. It is not only more difficult to make several slabs of the same size (the clay easily goes out of shape during cutting and removal), but rolled out slabs buckle more quickly than cut slabs.

Nameplate

◆ · · · ◆ · · · ◆ · · · ◆ · · · ◆ · · · ◆ · · · ◆

Use this new technique to create a nameplate, bearing either your name, or that of the person receiving the gift. Think about the design, and the extent of decoration and imagery. For the sake of this example, we will use the name W. Bumble, who lives in London.

The following equipment is required: roller; two battens of equal thickness; a new cloth; modelling tools; and a hole piercer. Use semi-plastic well-kneaded clay. Since white paint will be used, select white clay, and white slip.

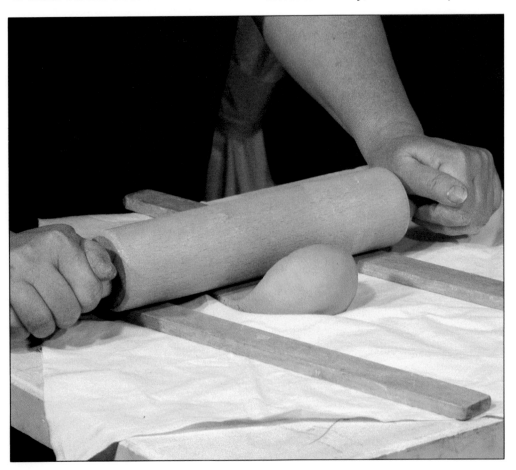

1 Cut off a piece of kneaded clay and shape it into a ball. Roll the clay out on the cloth between the wooden battens, which serve as a support. Occasionally turn the clay, which becomes progressively easy to work. The cloth absorbs any excess moisture, and can be washed, dried and reused. Next, place the rolled clay on the plaster board or a firm surface covered in newspaper to dry. Since paper and plaster are absorbent, the clay slab becomes more solid and does not lose its shape so quickly.

2 Next, cut a template out of paper. If the finished plate is to have specific dimensions, take into account shrinkage during drying and firing. Use the template to cut the shape out of the clay slab. Place this on the cloth. Meanwhile, the remaining clay is mixed together and briefly kneaded. Store it in a plastic cover so that it can be used again. Extra decorative pieces can be mounted with slip, though carved motifs are easier to make.

3 Apply the name using clay coils; mark it on the slab and then remove. Carve into the marked places, taking care not to apply too much slip afterwards.

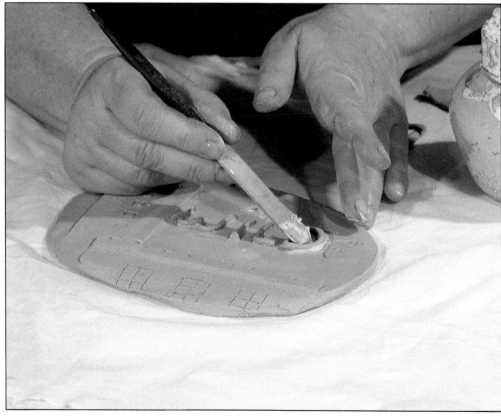

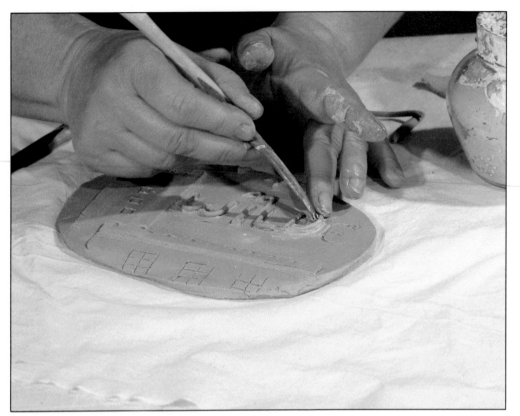

4 The name is fixed in place with light pressure. Carefully wipe and smooth away excess slip. If you want to paint the plate, study chapter 8, 'Forming the Surface'. Engobing (painting with earth colours) must be done now, while the clay is still damp.

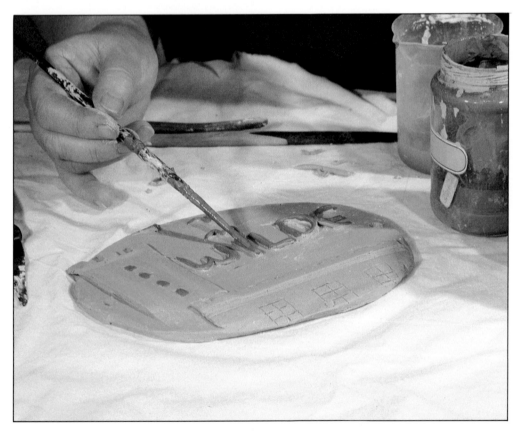

5 Do not forget the holes for screwing in the plate. When making these holes, cut right through the plate and clean the edges. As a test, stick a screw through (take shrinkage into account). If using two holes, align them carefully. Finally, the work is dried on a plaster board or board covered with newspaper. To prevent the slab from warping whilst drying, cover with a cloth.

Wall ornament

❖ ‥ ❖ ‥ ❖ ‥ ❖ ‥ ❖ ‥ ❖ ‥ ❖

This is a free-hanging piece, or large motif. The following equipment is required: paper templates for the motifs; roller; two thin battens; cloth; modelling tools; and slip. Use fine clay (light firing clay is easier to paint).

From the ball of clay roll out a thin slab. As always, do this on a cloth. Briefly leave the clay to dry. Then, cut out the shapes, lifting them carefully with a knife. Use your fingertips or modelling tools to smooth the edges afterwards.

Place the two identical shapes on the work table. Because the small piece of pottery is for hanging, both sides are the front and must therefore be decorated at the same time. Decorate regular shapes on their better side and irregular shapes in mirror image. After firing, stick the two pieces together and between them fix the string for hanging.

Both pieces are decorated by carving, stamping, or mounting pieces of clay.

Jewellery

❖ ‥ ❖ ‥ ❖ ‥ ❖ ‥ ❖ ‥ ❖ ‥ ❖

The success of jewellery depends on glazing and painting. They enable you to achieve great effects with simple shapes. The more imaginative you can be, the better. When making beads take care that the threading hole is big enough for the wire. The edges of these holes should be carefully cleaned and hollowed out. Be careful when making brooches – they should not be too thin, otherwise they will easily break. And remember that earrings should not be too heavy so that they can be worn comfortably.

1 You do not need many tools to make small pieces of jewellery apart from one or two modelling tools, and a needle for engraving and making holes in beads. Use clay containing fine fireclay.

2 If you wish to make beads you will also need fireproof wire. Beads are glazed all over and cannot therefore be laid in the kiln for firing. Instead they are hung on a wire. For brooches, you must purchase pins and a suitable adhesive in a handicraft shop.

Relief work

◆ ⋯ ◆ ⋯ ◆ ⋯ ◆ ⋯ ◆ ⋯ ◆ ⋯ ◆

The contrast between light and shadow, colour and black and white, and shiny and matt surfaces is very important. It creates tension which can be the subject of a specific item.

If you want to create a large relief work, big enough to cover a wall, it is advisable to make this out of small individual slabs, and to assemble them on a board after firing. Slabs which are too large suffer tensions during drying and firing, and easily crack. For this example we will choose a regular hexagon as the basic shape. Its advantage is that one piece can be added to another in a honeycombed shape, which can be extended and enlarged at will. Try out various techniques on the different parts for an amusing effect. The honeycomb piece is ideal for group work.

The following equipment is required: a roller; two wooden battens approximately 75cm (29in) thick; knife; slip; modelling tools; fork; and an assortment of shapes for stamping, such as screws, snail-shells, buttons, leaves, rings, indeed anything which leaves an imprint.

Up to a diameter of 15cm (5in) you can work in semi-plastic clay, but if you are starting with larger slabs, the fire-clay content must be higher. For this purpose, specialist shops offer 'slab clay'. The hexagon shape is not compulsory; a square is a reasonable alternative.

1 Cut a template of the basic shape. A hexagon is constructed as follows: with dividers make a circle and mark the radius at six points, then join these points together.

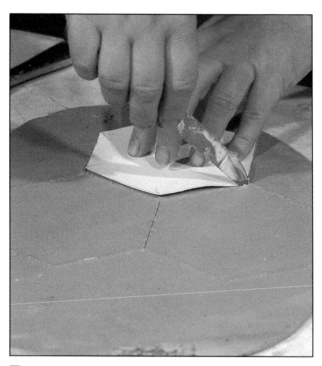

2 From the clay rolled out to a thickness of approximately 7–8mm (0.3in) cut 3–4 slabs.

3 The slabs are not worked on immediately, but packed airtight and put to one side for later use.

4 Smooth and trim all edges carefully.

5 On the slab to be worked, lightly mark a pattern. With screws, buttons, modelling tools or other objects the various motifs are imprinted.

6 With the next slab proceed differently, applying the motifs using strips, balls and spirals.

7 On the slab base, draw the pattern; carve along the drawn lines and apply slip, and with light pressure attach the pieces.

8 If the slabs are to be hung together, it is better if the patterns match.

9 On the third slab attach a tree shape.

10 Make the trunk from half a clay coil and press it on both sides into the slab with a modelling tool (do not forget to carve in and apply slip).

11 The top of the tree consists of single leaves – begin from the outside and work inwards. Attach the top in one piece and then add single branches with leaves.

12 An apple tree looks very good, particularly with apples amid the boughs and leaves.

13 The classical method of making a relief is by hollowing clay out of the slab. To do this take a thick slab so that it can be hollowed out up to 5–8mm (0.25in).

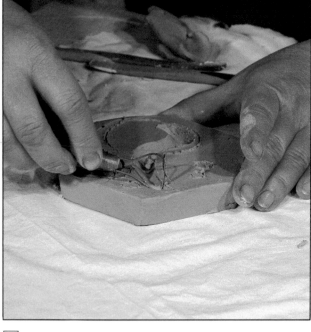

14 Sketch the motif and cut it out with the mirette. The clay is then smoothed out with modelling tools.

15 With the hexagon you can continue making pieces endlessly. For hanging, holes must be pierced.

RIGHT: **If you want to mount the slabs on a board, make hollows in the back where adhesive will form. Drill holes in the wooden board or chipboard, so the adhesive can also stick here.**

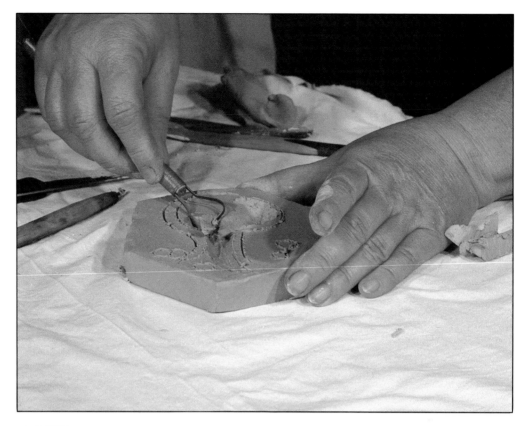

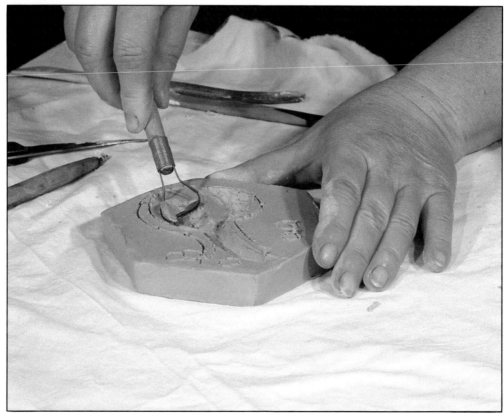

Teapot warmer

◆ ⋯ ◆ ⋯ ◆ ⋯ ◆ ⋯ ◆ ⋯ ◆ ⋯ ◆

As with the teapot, make a sketch plan. The warmer consists of the walls with openings which supply oxygen to the candle, and the lid on which the pot stands.

The following equipment is required. roller; two battens; knife; shape cutters; modelling tools; and slip. Use the same clay as used for the teapot.

1 You will need a roller, two battens, knife, shape cutters, modelling tools and slip. Use the same clay as for the teapot. From the rolled clay slab two round pieces of the same size are cut out. These will form the lid and the base, and are placed to dry on the plaster board or newspaper. When the base is solid, place a ring for the candle in the centre.

2 If the warmer is to be approximately 5cm (2in) high, cut a 5cm strip out of the rolled slab to form the casing (ie it must be as long as the circumference of the base). You can easily measure this by placing a piece of string around the base.

3 Cut decorative patterning in the casing and leave it to dry. Meanwhile, cut a hole in the lid through which the candle can be inserted, leaving enough edge for a small teapot to sit on.

4 Next, join the
casing to the base.
Roughen the edges
of the base and the
edges of the casing
(both lower and
upper edges, and on
the side for sealing
the casing).

5 Apply slip to the
base and attach the
casing. In the corner
joins place a thin coil
for stabilizing;
smooth it with a
modelling tool, first
towards the base
and then towards
the casing.

6 Seal the lateral joint by smoothing it with a knife. On the inside a strip of clay strengthens the join.

7 In the upper edge of the casing a clay coil is placed as a lid rest and coated with slip.

8 The lid is attached
with light pressure
and the join is
smoothed at the
edge.

Although used
for a traditional
purpose the teapot
need not be
traditional in design.

Lantern

◆ · · ◆ · · · ◆ · · · ◆ · · · ◆ · · · ◆ · · ◆ ·

Make a lantern following the previous technique. It can be hung up or put on the table. A lantern is constructed in such a way that one side gives out light and the other protects the light from wind and draughts. As a base choose any geometric shape – an oval, octagon or square. Since we have not yet made corner joins with slabs, choose a regular square. For the patient potter, a lantern built on a hexagonal base looks very beautiful.

For a square the following equipment is required: roller; battens; cloth; modelling tools; knife; a few leaves and blades of grass; fork for teasing the clay; and slip. Use semi-plastic light or white clay for the slabs.

First roll out a 5cm (2in) thick slab as large as possible. From this slab cut a square whose sides are approximately 8–10cm (3.5in) long. Then cut four lateral slabs with one side the same length as those of the square. The length of the other sides is determined by the height of the work to be made, let us say approximately 15–20cm (6–8in).

1 Two slabs keep the wind away, and have no openings for light. Begin with these two first. Put leaves and blades of grass on the still soft slabs, avoiding being too excessive. The leaves must be applied so that the ribs lie on the clay.

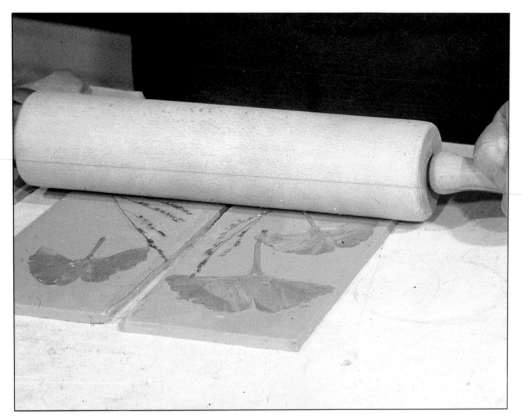

2 Carefully go over them with the roller, all together if possible. If it is easy, remove the leaves and grass. Very fine lines, now hardly visible, come to light on completion, so do not roll the leaves and grass with too much force. Any pieces not removed will fall out during drying, or burn in the kiln.

3 Next, cut a template for the slabs and cut around it. Before assembly check that all slabs are of the same size and match the base. The slabs are placed on the plaster board to dry partially. Then cut the openings into the remaining slabs. If these slabs have lost their shape whilst you have been working on them, cut back to the right size. Leave them on the plaster board to dry.

4 A small ring is fitted on the base slab, which holds the candle in place. In order to find the centre of the square, lay a piece of string in a cross from the corners. At the centre fix the ring for the candle. Cut the slabs to size. The corner joints are also cut at an angle. The base slab is teased and coated with slip all around.

Apply slip to the bevelled edge of two lateral slabs and mount one of them on the base. Hold this one fast and mount the other opposite. For the sake of stability, assemble these two slabs without openings first. Into all corner joints a strand of clay is placed and worked in, even in the join between the base and the wall. Now mount the third slab, coated with slip, and place clay coils in all the corners.

5 Smooth all joins before the last slab is inserted to prevent subsequent problems of access. Now insert the final slab and seal the remaining joins. If you wish to make a hanging lantern, pierce two or four holes. After firing thread a string or a chain through the holes for hanging.

If you have cut large or particularly filigree openings, handle the piece with special care.

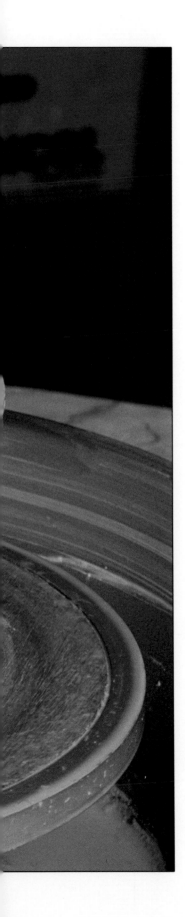

CHAPTER *seven*

◆·◆·◆·◆·◆·◆

Throwing and the Wheel

LEFT: **Once the basics are mastered, throwing on the potter's wheel offers endless varieties of shapes and forms.**

Working on the potter's wheel is a totally new experience and demands great patience and practice. Although it looks easy to master, it can take many hours before you produce the shapes you require. Note that an absolute must for throwing on the wheel is well-kneaded clay, free of air bubbles. Water is also used, though applied in a different way from 'hand building'. The hands are always kept damp, and a bucket of water must therefore be kept near the wheel. A sponge is also crucial to absorb excess water.

The following equipment is required: cutting wire; needle; mirette; sharp knife; a turning guide; and, of course, water and sponge.

Centring

◆·······◆·······◆·······◆·······◆·······◆·······◆

⬚1 Use well-kneaded throwing clay to shape a ball, about 1 kg (2.2lb) in weight. Throw this ball as near as possible to the middle of the wheel, which is turning in an anti-clockwise direction.

⬚2 Grasp the clay firmly, push it onto the wheel, and squeeze. By doing this the clay changes its shape and moves slightly upwards. Now hold the clay firmly with your left hand and press down with the right, immediately letting it move upwards again. Using the base of both palms the clay is pressed conically upwards.

⬚3 Repeat this process several times, until the clay runs smoothly between your hands and has stopped wobbling. While doing this, beware of any jerky movements, with hands or with the wheel. The clay is extremely plastic and reacts to any movement, instantly losing its shape. To get a safe hold, press both upper arms tight against your body.

Opening up

❖ ··· ❖ ··· ❖ ··· ❖ ··· ❖ ··· ❖ ··· ❖

Before opening up, the lump of spinning clay should be dome-shaped. With both thumbs press a hole in the middle, enlarging it with your left hand. If your hands are touching during this process, you can control them better. Work them down into the clay until you have reached the base. Take care while doing this, because you must be left with a base that is not too thin. If it is, it will break or distort on being removed from the wheel. Slowly stop the wheel to test the thickness of the base with a needle. If satisfied, set the wheel in motion again. If the base is too thin, it is best to start again from the beginning, since it is practically impossible to correct this problem. When the clay is spinning, pull it slowly outwards with the left hand to the desired diameter. With your thumbs in the opening, run both hands over the clay once more, and gently press the mass inwards again.

BELOW: **Rules need not always be followed to the letter: an edge which is left purposely 'unfinished' can be very effective.**

Lifting

◆ · · ◆ · · · ◆ · · · ◆ · · · ◆ · · · ◆ · · · ◆ · ·

Move your left hand into the clay to maintain the shape. With your right hand, or better with the knuckle of the index finger, carefully raise the height of the clay. Be careful, however, not to make the sides too thin. Repeat this process several times with smooth, flowing movements, to create a cylinder with walls of equal thickness. Whilst working, continually dampen your hands to lubricate the clay and prevent it from sticking to your fingers. If the clay should become dry, friction results and the piece loses its shape. As soon as the walls threaten to become too thin, draw the thumb and index finger of the left hand over them. In this way, the superfluous clay is removed and the walls will thicken.

Should you be unlucky enough to discover an air bubble, pierce the work with a needle. In bad cases, this may necessitate a fresh start.

◆ · · ◆ · · · ◆ · · · ◆ · · · ◆ · · · ◆ · · · ◆ · · · ◆ · · · ◆ · · · ◆ · · · ◆ · ·

1 Gradually the piece takes its form from the guidance of your left hand.

2 Be careful not to let the walls become too thin.

3 A bulbous shape is made by squeezing out a bulge in the cylinder from base to top.

Shaping

The easiest object to create is a *bowl*, since on the wheel the clay is automatically pushed outwards by centrifugal force. Ensure, however, that you always work from the bottom to the top, and never the reverse. Also check that your left hand shapes while the right gives constant counterpressure.

If the walls of the bowl widen too quickly they will begin to wobble and tear. Also take care that individual areas do not widen too far, or the walls will collapse because the clay above the weak points becomes too heavy.

RIGHT: **Putting the finishing touches to a bulbous bowl. Using the three basic techniques – cylinder, opening up and throwing inwards – you can create any conceivable shape.**

ABOVE: **If you want to narrow the shape at the top, grasp the cylinder with both hands and push the clay upwards applying gentle pressure. Not only will the diameter slowly decrease, but the walls will thicken automatically. Place the left hand inside, while the right presses lightly against it from outside to make the walls thinner.**

LEFT: **If you want to make a bulbous shape, first make the basic cylinder – narrow it at the top and proceed using your left hand by squeezing out the bulge from the bottom to the top. The right hand lightly guides the shape from the outside. To make a *jug* with a neck, create pressure with the right hand outside, guide the clay inwards, and throw a straight cylinder from the remaining clay to form the neck.**

Finishing

◆ · · · ◆ · · · ◆ · · · ◆ · · · ◆ · · · ◆ · · · ◆

Use a needle to make a hole in the upper wall of the piece. If the rim has become thin and uneven, the needle will remove the rim and cut a straight edge. The newly formed rim is run between two fingers, making it smooth and clean. With a sponge, preferably a natural one, go quickly over the outer layer and remove the collected slip, but be careful that you do not turn the work with the sponge. Next, absorb the water which has collected in the vessel with the sponge, and clean the wheel, again with the sponge. During this period the wheel is turning, but slowly. If you have finished and are satisfied with the result, stop the wheel. With taut cutting wire held close to the wheelhead, cut the work free. To guarantee that the piece comes away easily, pull the wire through two or three times. With your right hand carefully tilt the vessel into your left hand – do not use any force – and place it on a newspaper or a plaster board to dry. Any marks left by your hands are smoothed away with the sponge.

Spout

◆ · · · ◆ · · · ◆ · · · ◆ · · · ◆ · · · ◆ · · · ◆

If you want to use the thrown piece as a milk container or a jug, you must make a spout. Between the index finger and thumb of your left hand pull the rim outwards using the index finger of your right hand. Do this slowly or the rim will strain and tear.

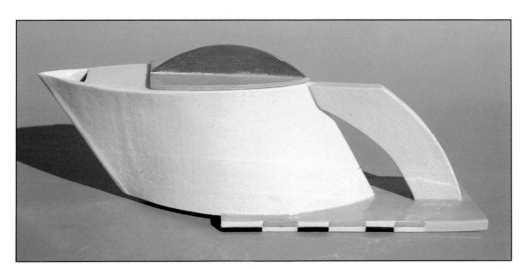

ABOVE: **A hand thrown bowl from Sante Fe, New Mexico.**

LEFT: **Here, the geometrical spout is integral to the overall design.**

Turning off

◆ ··· ◆ ··· ◆ ··· ◆ ··· ◆ ··· ◆ ··· ◆ ·

In order to obtain a smooth base, the vessel base is turned off, ie clay is removed and the underside is given its final shape. If you wish, you can turn and smooth the entire outer layer with a turning tool. When turning off, spiral patterns or rings can also be cut into the vessel. This is best done when the vessel is leather-hard (usually on the following day). Note that if the clay becomes too dry it crumbles away and small pieces can be torn out. If the work is too wet, the clay becomes lumpy and sticks to the turning tool.

LEFT: **Cutting spiral markings into a vessel while turning off.**

TOP: **To turn off, place the work with the opening down on the wheel. Make the wheel turn slowly and bring the shape into the centre. Then, fix it with small pieces of clay or a clay coil.**

BELOW LEFT: **If the vessel has a neck on which it will not stand safely, first throw a thick-walled cylinder and leave it to become leather-hard then place the vessel in this cylinder.**
   With the mirette, or a larger special metal turning tool, remove excess clay from the base and the underside. Small corrections to the shape can be made, as long as this does not affect the thickness of the walls. Finally, clean up with the damp sponge.

BELOW RIGHT: **When finished, let the piece dry. Since a lot of water is involved, the vessel needs longer to dry than the works made previously.**

Handle

◆ · · ◆ · · · ◆ · · ◆ · · · ◆ · · ◆ · · · ◆

If there is another part to be added to the thrown shape, such as a handle, attach it after turning off. Handles can be made in various ways. The simplest is to roll out a clay coil and attach this as a handle. Yet this has a disadvantage since stretching the clay, when bending it, causes cracks to form easily, making the handle fragile. Moreover, a flat handle looks better than a thick one.

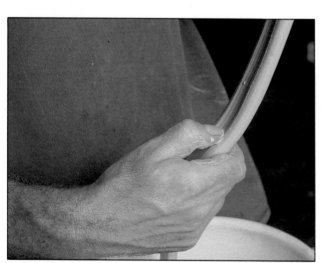

1 Stretch and smooth a clay coil to form a flat handle.

2 Mark the areas where the handle will be attached, then tease both places.

3 A conically shaped clay coil is placed on the work table, and is stretched and smoothed at the same time using water. Then cut the now flat strip of clay from the surface, hold it with your left hand, smooth it and pull it into the desired shape under running water with your right hand. Rinse your hands at the same time. Hang the strip of clay, now recognizable as a handle, over your right hand, and press the upper end onto the marked position.

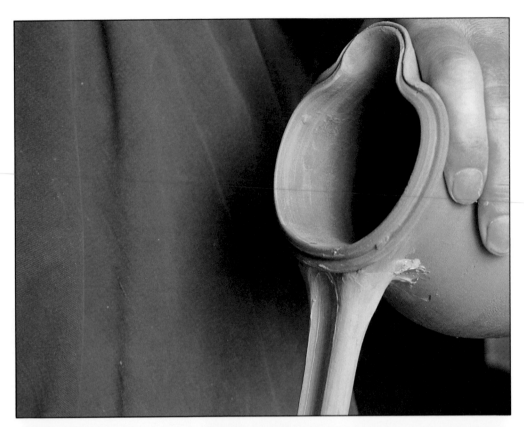

4 Press the lower end with your thumb into its place, squeezing off the surplus part of the strip. Clean the joints with a sponge or modelling tool. If you are not quite sure whether the handle will hold, use a small coil of clay to help. When attaching and smoothing the handle, its shape must not be damaged. Also take care that it does not lie above the rim of the vessel.

5 The better the line
and aesthetics, the
more an ordinary pot
can become a special
piece. One word of
caution though –
only hold the vessel
by its handle when it
has been through the
second firing.
Handles which have
broken off can no
longer be repaired.

CHAPTER *eight*

◆ · · ◆ · · ◆ · · ◆ · · ◆

Forming the Surface

RIGHT: **A brightly glazed selection of dinnerware. (Daphne Carnegy Ceramics.)**

RIGHT: **Hand-built,
burnished and
polished red clay
vase by Magdalene
Anyango Namakhiya
Odundo, 1985.**

No matter how perfect the shape of your pot or dish, the effect can all too easily be ruined by the wrong glaze or decoration. Although when first tackling these techniques it is very tempting to be ambitious, you will find that it is far safer to choose simple and straight-forward effects. They rarely fail. As you get more experience, so you can attempt larger effects. But without appreciating exactly what is involved in the following stages, you are unlikely to be successful.

Dark clays which contain manganese can be successfully and easily polished provided they are in a leather-hard condition. They require no glaze, having their own light and shadowy colour contrast. Glazes will, however, be required for white or light-firing clays. Light clays are best served by a simple decoration, covered with a transparent glaze. A general rule for beginners is to glaze light clay with light colours and dark clay with dark colours, so that the

LEFT: **Stoneware bowl
by Eric James Mellor,
UK. The design was
created by applying
basic oxides to
biscuit ware using a
water colourist's
painting technique.**

Ceramic colouring agents and glazes

◆　◆　◆　◆　◆　◆　◆　◆

RIGHT: **Burnished and decorated smoked dish by Siddig El Nigoumi, UK; it has been burnished with red slip and the decoration scratched through.**

BELOW: **Decorated earthenware plate by Ian McKenzie and Fiona Salazar, UK. The colours are mainly underglaze stains and glazes with some pink enamel onglaze.**

clay can shine through. Also note that when applying the glaze with a brush, the strokes will produce surface unevenness.

Patterns which have been carved in should never be covered with glaze because the pattern will lose its effect. If you wish to use colour, however, line the hollows with coloured engobe and use a transparent glaze.

ENGOBES

Engobes are extremely fine clay slips which are stained with oxides. Engobes are applied either to the leather-hard shape, or after biscuit firing. You can stain white clay slip by stirring up the slip from very fine pipe-clay, water and oxides. The addition of cobalt oxide produces blue engobe, iron oxide produces red engobe, chromium or copper oxide produces green engobe, and manganese oxide produces brown engobe. For reliable results, carry out test firings on small pieces of clay. In specialist shops ready-made engobes are available cheaply, mostly in powder form. To create shades within a colour add oxides or colouring agents.

The powders are mixed with water, and the consistency of the engobe should be milky to paste-like, according to your purpose. You may even wish to mix different engobes. Keep the mix in a sealed screw-top jar; but if, after a long period of time, it dries out or becomes too thick, add extra water.

Old earthenware jugs and bowls can be painted with engobe. Even today, rustic crockery is decorated with old patterns and motifs using earth colours, which are applied with a brush or slip trailer. The colouring agent is in the small rubber ball and, with light pressure, emerges through a pipette. Decorating with the slip trailer has an advantage over decorating with a brush. The biscuit-fired or leather-hard clay soaks up the water like a sponge and makes the brush become dry too

BELOW: **Glaze decorated stoneware bowl by Janice Tchalenko, UK. The biscuited bowl is decorated with a magnesia semi-shiny white glaze. When dry, coloured glazes are brushed and trailed onto the glaze.**

quickly. From the slip trailer, on the other hand, the colouring agent flows continuously and the patterns can be painted with a flowing stroke. The exceptions are plant parts, such as petals or short stalks. These look better if painted with a brush, since the colouring agent does not run out at an angle and a flourish can be better made with the wrist. Strokes also become more vivid when made with a brush. In both techniques, the consistency of the engobe is comparable to slightly thickened condensed milk.

There is another use for engobe, besides painting – a finished work can be partly or completely stained in a clay colour. The engobe is poured over the work, and the coloured area is then 'tidied up' with a brush. Note that when the engobe was applied with a brush it had the consistency of thick milk; now when it is poured over the work it should have the consistency of thin milk (this can easily be achieved through the addition of water). Works treated with engobe only obtain their radiant colour through a transparent glaze which is applied after biscuit fir-

ing. Pouring the engobe over the artifact is a new variation in the process. Also, carving patterns into the places where engobe has been poured and which have been stained, enables the colour of the clay to emerge.

When engobing the interior of a bowl, or other hollow items, pour the liquid into the middle and spin the colouring agent briskly round the vessel with a rotating movement. It is poured out over the rim, making sure that there are no overlaps of colour. Since engobes are fine earths with a high melting point, they do not melt and run during firing. This means, however, that overlaps are equivalent to an intensification in colour which can, from time to time, create attractive effects.

When colouring the exterior, hold the vessel with its face down, and pour over the liquid with a smooth rotating movement of the other hand. However, many pieces of work are so big that they cannot be held with one hand. In order to pour engobe over these pieces, place them on two wooden battens (again with the opening pointing down) over a bucket. In this way they can be easily coated by pouring slowly but steadily. Smaller pieces of work can be completely dipped into the colouring agent – hold the piece firmly in two inconspicuous spots and slide it briskly through the glaze. The places where you held the piece are painted over with a brush. Note that dipping should only be carried out on fired pieces since unfired clay can absorb too much moisture, swell, and finally crack. Also, both techniques, pouring and dipping – are preferable to painting with a brush, since after firing any irregularity, no matter how small, becomes visible and a brush always leaves marks.

When applying engobe to an unfired and a fired piece, the one major difference is that the colour and intensity is greater on the latter, and the engobe looks more radiant. Structures can therefore be more clearly emphasized in this way.

There are just two real mistakes to avoid during engobing. The first occurs if applying the engobe too thickly, for it flakes off or becomes cracked. The second problem occurs when you have a greasy or dusty surface, because colours will not 'take'. An item can become

greasy if it is left to stand for too long and is frequently handled. However, this grease can be completely removed by a second biscuit firing. Dust can usually be easily rinsed off (when the piece has been fired). One final possible problem involves decorations – using a blue flower, for instance, instead of a red one. The error should be wiped off with a cloth or removed with a knife after drying. Fortunately, since the colours are non-toxic, easy to handle, and not too expensive, children can also use them, which is not always the case with other decorative techniques.

METAL OXIDES

Metal oxides have been used in ceramics since ancient times, and are the colouring agent for these products. Their advantage lies in the fact that their colouring power is not lost at high temperatures, and in fact sometimes only appears during the firing stage. Oxides are also valued because they supply the colouring for glass, and can be used as a stained underglaze or overglaze.

The most important oxides for potters are cobalt – which produces a blue tint; iron – yellow-red to red-brown; and copper – blue-green. (If they are reduced, ie fired with insufficient oxygen, copper produces a red colour.) Manganese produces a dark brown to brownish violet, while tin is a white clouding agent. White glazes, which contain tin oxide, form the base for faience painting. Chromium oxide gives a green colour. One of the most important oxides for glaze production is lead oxide, which not only gives colour, but raises the fusibility of glazes, giving them transparency and brilliance. Interestingly, glass makers also use lead for these reasons.

With lead compounds being mostly toxic, they are only available in the form of frits from manufacturers. In frits, water-soluble materials are melted with silica to produce insoluble silicates. However, the poison can emerge from the fired clay after contact with acids. Consequently you must not use any lead-containing glazes for ceramics. Also note that from a firing temperature of 1,140°C (2,084°F) the lead no longer has any effect. In glass which contains lead, it is so firmly bound that it loses its toxicity.

LEFT: **Stoneware platter by Milton Moon, Australia. A sensitive rendering of inglaze brushwork on an oxidised stoneware platter. Decoration is with basic oxides on to a nephyline syenite glaze.**

BELOW: **Decorated white glaze jar by Daphne Carnegie, UK. An opaque white glaze is used as a base; basic oxides were used for decorating, but were mixed together with a little of the basic glaze and red stain, and some extra glaze for the red spots.**

RIGHT: **Porcelain vessel by Robin Hopper of Canada. Thrown form with thrown clay additions. It is glazed with an alkaline slip glaze with additions of copper and rutile.**

RIGHT: **Porcelain vessel by Robin Hopper of Canada. Thrown form with thrown clay additions. It is glazed with an alkaline slip glaze with additions of copper and rutile.**

BELOW: **Raku dish by David Miller, UK. After biscuit firing it was coated with copper slip and rapidly fired to 1,830°F (980°C), then subjected to reducing and smoking in a metal container.**

As will be clear, handling oxides requires some practice. First attempts with glazes can be made with those which we stain with oxides. In order to obtain precise results, the glaze to oxide ratio should be written down and recorded with test firings. For beginners, however, this is hardly a suitable method. When painting under the glaze or on top of it, the beginner should decide to use prepared colours which are easier to handle and yield better results.

Underglaze colours

Underglaze colours are used for painting directly on to the biscuit-fired surface. If it is coated with engobe, you can paint on this as well. This is the stage where clay is also coated with transparent glaze.

Underglazes are available in powder form or ready-made in small bowls. If using the former, which is usually slightly better value, mix it with dextrin or wallpaper paste. In the absence of either, thick sugar water is sufficient as a binding agent. Do beware, however, of simply mixing coloured pigments with water, because they do not adhere to the clay surface so well, and they will run when the transparent glaze is applied.

The ready-made colours are applied as a water solution and can be treated as water colours. Apply several test brush strokes to gauge the colour, and find out to what extent the clay absorbs the moisture (always far more rapidly than paper will). The colours can be mixed with each other, giving a palette of various shades. Mixing is done on a sheet of glass.

When choosing brushes do not make false economies – a good sable-hair brush makes the work considerably easier. Conversely, a bad brush can easily spoil the enjoyment of working. The pointed brush, soaked with colour, is swiftly but smoothly drawn over the clay surface. The colours can be used very sparingly, since they only obtain their intensity when being fired with the transparent. If you make a mistake, it can be washed out, but this is some-

times difficult if the colour has soaked too far into the clay. If the mistake is very obtrusive, the entire decoration must be washed off. Prior to restarting the work, the damp clay is dried. Incidentally, it is also worth considering buying finished tiles, plates and other unpainted pieces. All are very suitable for painting because they are cast, and therefore have a very smooth surface.

After painting, pour transparent glaze over the piece to give the colours their intensity and brilliance. When buying colouring agents for underglaze painting do note the temperature up to which these can be fired. If you exceed these levels, the colours could burn. In higher firing temperatures many colours tend to fade.

FAR LEFT: **Ceramic pencils and crayons make it possible to draw illustrations and lettering on biscuit ware with freedom and precision. These mugs are by Ann Clark, UK.**

LEFT: **Egyptian paste bottle by Dick Studley, USA. Stabilized stains are used to colour clay. If the basic oxides of copper manganese are used the effect is much softer.**

BELOW: **Showing the range of underglaze colours available for painting on to biscuitware. The colours have been stabilized, so that they will not soften and fuse with the glaze when fired.**

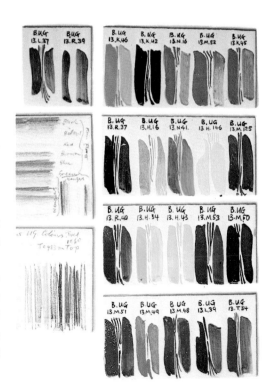

BELOW: **Thrown bone china and coloured glaze pieces by Kenneth Clark, UK. Clear and semi-opaque coloured earthenware glazes have taken on added luminosity during the firing process.**

Onglaze colours

◆ · · · ◆ · · · ◆ · · · ◆ · · · ◆ · · · ◆ · · · ◆

Both majolica and faience painting are described at the beginning of the book. Ceramic colours are painted on to a white tin glaze. The colours blend with the glaze, and penetrate, but do not run into it. They will not remain as hard as underglaze colour.

If painting under the glaze on to the clay surface was quite simple, painting on the glaze is not so easy. You should practise on test pieces.

When painting on the unfired glaze note the sole possibility for correction consists in washing the whole piece of work, which is not always possible for large pieces.

Majolica colours are available in powder form in specialist shops. The colours can be mixed with one another. Since the colour is immediately absorbed by the glaze, it is sufficient to mix the powder with water.

The consistency of the colour must be right – if it is too liquid, it can run over the glaze, and 'holes' form in the surface. If the colour is mixed too thick, it sits on the surface and produces a dull effect.

Mix the colours in small quantities on a glass or porcelain palette, and carefully add water drop by drop. Stir in the colouring agent with a small knife. The mixed colour should not run on the palette, but be moist enough to avoid being lumpy.

A white glaze is applied to the fired clay surface, preferably by pouring. Before painting the work, it must be cleaned, to ensure there is no glaze sticking to the base. And, by now, any irregularities on the glaze should have been removed. The work can now only be touched with great care, although on no account may the painted surfaces be touched at all. Begin by adding just one colour, mixing in others later. If you are feeling brave, you can also try using an oxide.

RIGHT: **Stoneware vase with a sparkling aventurine glaze by Henri Simmen. Ivory stopper.**

BELOW LEFT: **A vivid fruit-patterned plate by Britain's best-known ceramics designer, Clarice Cliff.**

Painting with vitrifiable colours

Vitrifiable colours offer a further means of decorating ceramics. These colours are applied to the glazed and fired clay surface at low temperatures, being fused on to the glaze in a separate firing at 600°–900°C (1,112°–1,652°F). Vitrifiable colours are available for purchase as powders, which are mixed with thick oil on a glass or porcelain palette. They can be mixed with each other to provide different shades of colour.

The painting technique is relatively simple, and corrections can be easily made. It is best to paint with a fine brush. In addition to the vitrifiable colours, a gold lustre can also be fused on to the glaze. This lustre is, admittedly, very expensive because it consists of a solution of pure gold, but you can use it sparingly to achieve beautiful effects. With vitrifiable colours you can also also paint fired porcelain. And, as has already been mentioned, there is almost no restriction in the choice of colours.

Glazing

◆ ⋯ ◆ ⋯ ◆ ⋯ ◆ ⋯ ◆ ⋯ ◆ ⋯ ◆

This is the most important subject in ceramic decoration. The word glaze is related to the word glass and in fact the raw materials of both are very similar. Since glaze is ground, prepared glass, it is not surprising that glass and ceramic manufacture often follow the same lines.

Glass is a very old Germanic word. When glass became well known during the Bronze Age in central Europe, in the form of beads and jewellery, this new glittering material reminded people of the well known amber, which was then called 'glasa', the 'shimmerer'. This name was passed on to the new sub-

stance, which has ever since been known as glass. Glazes are however not merely decorative since they also protect the clay surface, make it water-impermeable, give it smoothness and colour and make it harder and therefore more resistant to impact.

GLAZE BUYING

There are transparent, colourless glazes, as well as matt, gloss, covering and crystal-forming types. And, through constant development, new glazes are constantly being created. Samples usually come in the form of small clay tablets, including six different types of white, and a range of other colours from yellow to green. And note that a brown glaze gives a reddish hue on dark clay, whilst on white clay it is almost yellow.

The easiest glazes to handle are the ready-mixed kind. They are expensive and available in tins; they will reliably produce the same colour each time. They can be applied immediately with the brush and any irregularities in the application of colour disappear during firing. The glazes can also be mixed with each other, or alternatively you can apply the colours side by side or as patterns (eg spots with a second colour which will run into the glaze underneath). Superb effects can be achieved with these ready-made glazes.

Conventional glazes are available in powder form, and must be mixed with water. First, however, you must differentiate between lead-free glazes and those which contain lead. The latter, incidentally, offer a better colour range because lead glazes are considerably easier to manufacture.

Glazes which contain lead can only be used for decorative ceramics, just like

LEFT: **Thrown lustre bowl by Margery Clinton, UK. After biscuit-firing, the bowl was glazed with a tin glaze, Prepared salts of silver or copper mixed with glaze are applied with a sponge to the unfired glaze.**

BELOW: **Stoneware and porcelain bowls by Lucy Rie, UK, showing a range of possible high-temperature yellows. (Left) this bowl is thrown porcelain with a transparent ceranium yellow glaze. A porcelain body (right) with a transparent yellow glaze is used for another bowl, and a yellow-stained barium matt glaze is used on a stoneware body (centre).**

glazes containing cadmium or selenium (cadmium glazes are yellow, selenium glazes are red). Next, consider the firing temperature. Earthenware should be fired at 1,000°–1,060°C (1,832°–1,940°F), stoneware at 1,100°–1,300°C (2,012°–2,372°F). The glazes fired at lower temperatures are more colourful. At higher firing temperatures, however, all glazes are fast and can therefore be used for holding food, but the colour range is clearly reduced. Yet we can still choose between matt, gloss, transparent, and opaque glazes.

For beginners, try using lower temperatures when firing earthenware. The material behaves predictably in firing, although it can still surprise. The most important glaze is transparent,

which is also usually the cheapest. For pieces of jewellery and other decoration use a lead-glaze, which offers a more brilliant shine. It should also be used for all interior glazes on tableware, being not only non-toxic but appetizing in appearance. The final point is that pieces which are painted with engobe or underglaze colour are coated with transparent glaze. If you wish to experiment, stain them with oxides.

As a second glaze you can try a simple white one, which can be used in many different ways. You can paint on it, stain it with colouring agents, or leave it as a white glaze. If you decide on a further glaze, take advice as to whether the glaze is easily applied and suitable. Do not be dazzled by the beautiful col-

ours – choose a glaze which can easily be worked. Later, when you are slightly more experienced, you can use a greater range of colours.

PREPARATION OF THE GLAZE

Mix the glaze with water until the substance has the consistency of condensed milk. Apply the glaze the day before use, to save time later. Note that when pouring the powder into a bucket, a face mask should be worn, if possible. The water is then poured on to the powder, approximately 1l (1.76 pints) to 1kg (2.2lbs) of glaze. The mixture is stirred with a wooden stick or an old stirring spoon and then sieved. This is advisable, even if the glaze is not lumpy. Keep it in sealable containers, and should it ever dry out add water ensuring the liquid is well mixed. Note that some glazes sink rapidly to the bottom, necessitating the purchase of glaze suspenders which prevent or significantly slow this process. Also note that some glazes will not tolerate frost, so store in a frost-free place.

GLAZE TESTING

In order to understand glazes, you should prepare small tablets of clay, number them, and conduct test firings. Keep a record in an exercise book of the results, observing how the glazes react to decorative colours, how they mix with engobes, and how they behave on different coloured clays. You should also fire them at varying temperatures. It is best to fire one tablet flat and one standing and note how the glaze runs (with some glazes there are significant differences). This test procedure is invaluable, ensuring major mistakes do not afflict important items, spoiling the work prior to this stage.

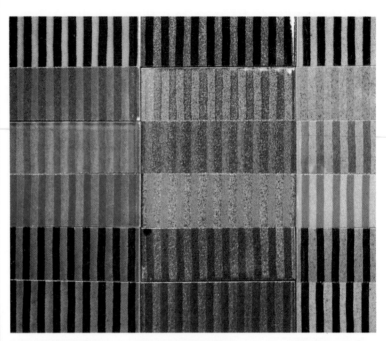

Brown green glaze　　**Burnt Sienna glaze**　　**Pale brown glaze**

GLAZE APPLICATION

Glaze can be applied in many different ways, the easiest domestic method involving a brush. However, do not try to paint with the brush (preferably bristle and 2cm [½in] wide). The glaze mixture should be applied swiftly in one direction. Since the fired clay quickly absorbs moisture, use a brush which holds the water for as long as possible. In specialist shops you will find an immense choice of such brushes.

If you want to glaze a hollow body, first rinse out the inside with glaze, preferably the transparent kind. This should be mixed thinly. If some of the inside glaze runs on to the outside, it can easily be wiped off when dry, because the clay quickly absorbs water and the glaze sticks to the ceramic like powder. Finally the glaze is applied to

ABOVE: **In this illustration, the stripes were printed by silk screen directly onto the tile. When dry they were spray-glazed with transparent coloured glazes. This demonstrates the range of effects from different glazes.**

the exterior. The thickness of the glaze is approximately 0.3–1.5mm ($\frac{1}{100}$in). In addition to applying it with a brush, there are other ways. The piece can be dipped in the glaze, the glaze can be poured over it, or you can use a spray gun. Note, however, that in addition to the gun you will need a special booth.

When using the dipping process carefully but firmly hold the piece in your hand, and quickly dip it into the glaze. Then, lift it out to drip over the glaze bucket. If you have a hollow body to glaze in this way, hold it upside down so that the glaze does not run in from the outside. A larger vessel can be held with glazing tongs, but this requires some practice. During dipping the clay easily soaks up water, and the glaze mixture becomes thick, so it must therefore be thinned from time to time. If you are working with a pottery group this dipping technique can easily be used because of the availability of large quantities of glaze.

An alternative glazing technique, which is popular and easily managed at home, involves glazing through pouring. If you have a work which is not too big, and which can be held in one hand, hold it by the base and pour the glaze over whilst gently rotating the piece.

If, however, the piece is so big or so heavy that it cannot easily be held in one hand, place two wooden battens over the glaze bucket and place the piece on top (hollow bodies upside down). Use a ladle to pour the glaze over the work.

If you have a banding wheel, place it under the bucket so that the bucket and the work can be rotated together. In this way the glaze is applied neatly and effortlessly. And finally, note that if transparent glazes are applied twice in

RIGHT: **A pure, unadulterated blue glaze is subtly edged in gold.**

some places, this produces interesting effects.

CLEANING UP

The base of the work must be carefully wiped so that it does not stick to the fireclay plate in the kiln. It is also advisable to keep the bottom 2–3mm ($\frac{1}{10}$in) free of glaze, so that if the glaze does run you can avoid troublesome drips on the base. Also note, when glazing, that glazes are delicate and absolute cleanliness is crucial. A separate brush must be used for each glaze. To avoid getting dust on the glaze, cover the glaze bucket with a lid after use.

Remaining glazes can be collected in an extra container, as can the glaze dust which arises when you wipe the work. These mixed glazes are sometimes quite delightful, but cannot be introduced into your mixture. They are, however, always useful for glazing the inside surfaces of pieces.

And finally, do ensure that you protect yourself. Glaze particles are sharp-edged, as indicated by quickly worn thin brushes and worn-out wooden stirring spoons. Do not therefore breathe in glaze dust, and wear a face mask when mixing glazes. Nor should you eat, smoke or drink whilst working. Since glazes can also contain toxic substances, you should always wear rubber gloves.

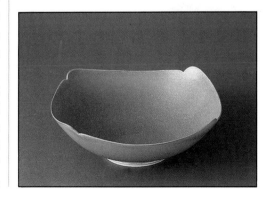

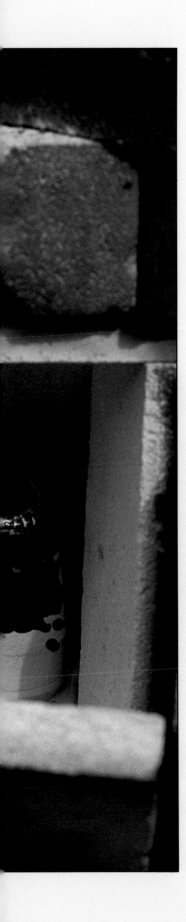

CHAPTER *nine*

◆······◆·····◆·····◆·····◆·····◆

Firing

LEFT: **Pots being fired
in the kiln.**

Biscuit firing

◆ · · ◆ · · ◆ · · ◆ · · ◆ · · ◆ · · ◆

Clay obtains its strength through firing, with malleable clay being transformed into a solid ceramic. In the heat of the fire the clay sinters, which means that its minerals fuse and solidify.

Two firings are necessary in order to make ceramics covered with glaze, from the greenware. With biscuit firing, the ware is prepared for glazing, although theoretically a first firing is not necessary. Some manufacturers avoid this, believing that the glaze penetrates unfired glazed clay more effectively. For domestic purposes, however, it is easier to work on the clay after biscuit firing, since the unfired ware is very fragile and easily broken.

Biscuit fire at 900°C (1,382°F). At this temperature the clay is solid, but still sufficiently porous for the glaze to adhere. The final temperatures should be arrived at gradually, since chemical transformations take place during firing. The first critical phase is at 200°–300°C (392°–572°F), the second at about 600°C (1,112°F). There are particles in the clay which begin to vitrify at these temperatures, and stick the substances together. Since these chemical reactions put a strain on the work, these should be approached slowly.

BELOW: **Showing the use of tongs to move pots in the kiln.**

TEMPERATURE ADJUSTMENT AND FIRING

A wide variety of electronically controlled kilns, in which you only need set a program are now available. There are at least two programs, one for biscuit firing and the other for glaze firing. There are, additionally, manufacturers who offer programs which can operate more complex firing cycles. Such kilns have very reliable temperature controls, and a sensor measuring the degree of heat in the kiln.

In less sophisticated kilns, which have no electronic controls, the temperature is measured with pyrometric cones (three-sided thin pyramids). They are made in such a way that they will melt and bend at a given temperature. Three cones are placed in an observation window in the kiln, where they can easily be seen. The middle cone is linked to the temperature required for firing and begins to lose its shape when the desired temperature is reached. The cone before it is for a lower temperature, and will by this stage have already fallen. The third cone will fall at a higher temperature. These cones are obtainable in grades from 600° to 2,000°C (1,112° to 3,632°F).

Electronic kilns, in which it is only necessary to select and set a program, are extremely expensive. However, there

BELOW: **Glazing a piece after the initial biscuit firing.**

are kilns in which temperature, heat output, and holding time of the temperature reached must be set at the beginning of the firing. They automatically control the temperature and will switch off at the required moment.

For the first firing phase up to 300°C (572°F) you need a heat output of only 20–30 per cent. At this most critical stage the remaining water is also expelled from the work. If there is still too much moisture in the work, unable to escape, there will be an explosion in the kiln. The second firing phase, up to approximately 600°C (1,112°F), is reached with about 50–60 per cent heat output. Often there is a time switch built in for this second firing stage. Select from four to six hours for sensitive and thick pieces of work, and two to four hours for other, more basic pieces. The third firing phase, up to 900°C (1,652°F) can be achieved with the full output of the kiln. The pieces are already solid, and all moisture will have evaporated. This temperature is held for about 20 minutes. Since electronic kilns control and regulate these firing stages automatically, they are obviously an asset. If possible, try to use one.

Packing the kiln

To make the best possible use of space in the kiln, you will need to add shelves. These can be made from refractory tiles and kiln props, tiles being available in a range of sizes. For intermediate layers which do not take up the entire base of the kiln, use one or two half-tiles. It is also possible to use tiles with holes, which heat more rapidly since they have less mass, and therefore use up less electricity. However, these tiles

have two disadvantages: they are fragile and break easily; and if, during glaze firing, the works are too thickly glazed, the substance can drip on to items situated below.

For plates and tiles, shelves are available on which they can be placed to save space. Since in biscuit firing glazes do not melt and the pieces cannot stick together, smaller items can be placed inside larger ones. Extreme caution is advised, however, when doing this, because the pieces are easily broken. Do not carry pieces by their handles, but lift and support them. Also, avoid placing heavy pieces on top of thin, light, fragile pieces. Never try to cram too many small items inside a larger one, and remember that openings can shrink during firing. It is very tempting to place flat tiles inside other pieces, since they are particularly difficult to pack. But they are also among the most sensitive pieces at this firing stage. Such tiles are best placed flat in such a way that they will take up little room.

It is very important that there is good air circulation within the kiln. The best place, therefore, for flat pieces is in the middle of the kiln. Round pieces usually survive firing without any problems, and can be placed anywhere. You should also try to place pieces of similar height together. Small pieces are situated on the lowest level, with kiln props. They must reach at least 3–4mm (1/10in) above the highest piece of work, so that the heavy fire clay bat does not crush the greenware. This can easily be checked with a wooden batten, moving from one prop to another.

If you build on three props, the bat resting on them cannot wobble since it will be well supported. The props are arranged in a triangle, and should as far

FACING PAGE: **A kiln constructed out of doors may sometimes be convenient, though offers only a primitive facility.**

as possible be situated at the outer edge of the bat and be evenly distributed on the surface. In a round kiln this three-point construction is ideal. If you have a large square kiln to pack, the best technique is to build on four props in the corners.

The fire clay bat is placed on the kiln props, which is occasionally hard work in big kilns, since it is essential to work with the utmost caution. If you accidentally knock any delicate piece it will almost certainly be fractured beyond repair.

If the kiln is large enough, you can insert several bats. Note, however, that on inserting the props and bats, the former must always stand directly above one another, otherwise the bats become unevenly loaded and may break.

If at the end there remain a few tall pieces which will not make an entire layer, insert a 'mezzanine' using a small or half-bat. Be careful though. The greenware which is being placed in the kiln is raw, and very sensitive. Hold such items in both hands to avoid any accidents. And if a piece does not easily fit in do not force it. Wait for the next firing.

When the kiln is properly filled, it is closed and firing can commence. Since most modern kilns have a temperature indicator, you can see when it drops to approximately 200°C (392°F), at which point the kiln can be carefully opened a little. Do not open until the gauge indicates this temperature since cooling causes items to contract, putting a strain on and resulting in cracks. At a temperature of approximately 100°C (212°F) the items can be removed from the kiln (you may wish to wear gloves to protect your hands).

Glaze firing

In glaze firing, as the term indicates, the glaze is melted on to the biscuit pot. During this firing process the glaze melts, becomes liquid, and burns into the ware as a permanent layer. The hardness of the ceramics is determined by this temperature.

FIRING TEMPERATURES
● Earthenware (for example tableware and ornamental ceramics) is fired at a temperature of 1,040–1,060°C (1,904–1,940°F).
● Stoneware, including dinner services, wall plaques and washing bowls, is fired at a temperature of approximately 1,250°C (2,282°F).
● Fine ceramics for crockery, floor tiles, insulators and acid-resistant containers, are fired at a temperature of 1,300°C (2,372°F).
● Coarse stoneware encompasses sewage pipes, clinker bricks, troughs, pickle jars, and beer mugs, and is fired at 1,000°C (1,830°F).

Salt glaze is also fired at this temperature. During firing, rock salt is thrown into the kiln. The resulting vapours produce the typical transparent silky matt shine of this ware. Salt glazes cannot be used in electric kilns, however, since the elements would burn out during this process.
● Porcelain needs a temperature of 1,350–1,460°C (2,462–2,660°F). Porcelain is the hardest, most robust utility ceramic.

For the best results, purchase both clay and glaze in the same shop. This will ensure that both elements are suited to each other.

FACING PAGE: **Once fired, the pot should be allowed to cool.**

Firing and cooling

If the glazed pieces are placed dry in the kiln, you can fire them with full heat output. If the pieces are still rather damp, for the first half hour or so they should be fired at reduced output. Also note that items are under strain both during firing and cooling. The latter should not therefore take place abruptly. Only open the kiln at low temperatures, and remove the objects when they have completely cooled down.

FILLING THE KILN

This stage, before glaze firing, is done with the utmost care. No piece can touch another, no 'towers' can be built, and there can be no contact with the walls of the kiln or the elements. Each item must stand alone and the air must be able to circulate freely. Pieces of the same height are grouped together.

All pieces must have a clean base, yet it can be hard to avoid a drop of extra glaze. Sometimes the glaze runs and drips, joining a piece to a bat. To avoid freeing the two using a hammer and chisel, place items on stilts or saddles. When the first layer has been constructed, install a bat above it and put in the second layer. If, despite due care, a drop of glaze falls on to the bat, remove this with a hammer and chisel immediately after cooling. Such difficulties can however be avoided if you coat the bat beforehand with a separating agent. The glaze can then be easily removed using a spatula. The hole in the protective coating should immediately be painted over.

ABOVE: **A selection of brightly glazed dinner ware. (Daphne Carnegie Ceramics)**

OPPOSITE: **With knowledge of the basic techniques of pottery, and imagination, there is no limit to the designs that can be created, as this extraordinary teapot illustrates.**

Index

Picture Credits

Visual Arts Library: pages 65, 84, 91, 96, 115, 125.
Daphne Carnegie Ceramics: pages 102, 124.
Every effort has been made to contact copyright holders, and the publisher apologises for an omissions that may have been made.